Opening Your Door to Children: How To Start a Family Day Care Program

Kathy Modigliani
Marianne Reiff
Sylvia Jones

A 1986–1987 *Comprehensive* Membership Benefit

**NATIONAL ASSOCIATION FOR THE
EDUCATION OF YOUNG CHILDREN
WASHINGTON, DC 20009-5786**

National Association for the Education of Young Children
1834 Connecticut Avenue, N.W.
Washington, DC 20009-5786
202-232-8777   800-424-2460

Library of Congress Catalog Card Number: 87-060747

ISBN Catalog Number: 0-935989-06-4

NAEYC #203

Printed in the United States of America

Acknowledgments

Many people have helped with this handbook, especially:

Child Care Coordinating and Referral Service (4 C's)
University of Michigan Family Housing Services
Students of the CCCRS-UMFH Day Care Homes Project
The Day Care Homes Association of Washtenaw County

Bill Kell
Bess Manchester
Sandy Settergren
Mary Wehking
Anthony Barker
Miriam Rosado
Joan Kauffman
Marlene Atkins
John Reiff
Ruth Booth
LaVerna Calloway Cash
Liz Alery
Ken Moore
Lander McLoyd

Eileen Cottington
Helene Mayleben
Marie Bowles
Debbie Schultz Grady
Laverne Jackson-Barker
Karen Jania
Ruth Freedman
Kerry Olson
Betty Hardee
Maryann Morris
Judith Schmitt-VanBuren
Liz Jewell
Jacquelyn Wood
Alejandra Morua

The CCCRS-UMFH Day Care Homes Project was sponsored by:

The Child Care Coordinating and Referral Service*
408 N. First Street
Ann Arbor, MI 48103
313-662-1135

* with funding from the
City of Ann Arbor Community Development Block Grant

and

University of Michigan Family Housing Services
1588 Cram Circle
Ann Arbor, MI 48105
313-763-1440

Contents

PART 1. DECIDING TO START

PART 2. PARENTS

PART 3. FAMILY DAY CARE IS A SMALL BUSINESS

PART 4. YOUR PROGRAM

PART 5. YOU AS A PROFESSIONAL

INTRODUCTION

This handbook introduces you to family day care. We hope we can help you decide whether or not being a child care provider is a good occupation for you. If you decide to begin a program of your own, you will find helpful suggestions for planning and preparation. If you are already caring for children, it may help you improve your service.

You will not find many ideas for daily activities here—that would require another whole book! However, the Bibliography includes books on program ideas you may want to try after you open your door to children.

When we train new family day care pro-

viders, we find people frequently ask the same questions, so we wrote the first edition of this handbook to answer those questions. Since then, we have made revisions based on suggestions from other providers and our years of experience. Throughout the text you will find the names of some providers in our classes who have offered good suggestions. We will continue to revise this handbook, making changes as suggested by our readers. If you have ideas for additions or changes, please send them to NAEYC's editorial department. Your name will be acknowledged if your suggestions are used.

Definitions

A **family day care provider** offers care in her or his own home to a small group of children. In most states, family day care is limited to six or fewer children. This type of care is sometimes referred to as *home child care.*

A **group child care provider** offers child care in her or his own home to a larger group of children. In most states, group care is limited to 12 or fewer children, and at

least one assistant must be present. In some states, you must have a license for a child care center to care for more than 6 children.

For simplicity, this handbook will use the terms *family day care* to refer to both types of in-home care settings, and *family day care provider,* or *home child care provider,* to refer to the caregiver.

The need for family day care programs

More than one half of all mothers with preschool children now work outside the home. This is three times as many as 30 years ago. The most rapid increase has been in working mothers of children younger than age 3—in fact, 48% of all mothers of children younger than 1 year old are in the workforce (Bureau of Labor Statistics, 1986). Many parents of infants and toddlers prefer a home setting for the care of their children.

The latest figures for the number of working families who use family day care are from the Current Population Survey (Bureau of the Census, 1983). This survey found the following information for children younger than 5 cared for in another's home:

Mother working full time
    Cared for by a nonrelative   24.1%
    Cared for by a relative   19.7%
Mother working part time
    Cared for by a nonrelative   18.4%
    Cared for by a relative   15.7%

Unfortunately, the Bureau of the Census does not keep figures on working fathers, or on the use of family day care by nonworking parents.

According to the Congressional Budget Office, by 1990 an additional 2.5 million children will require some form of child care. Because parents prefer family day care, especially for their younger children, we can expect to see an increasing demand for years to come.

According to the Internal Revenue Service, in 1983, 6.4 million families received a total of $2.6 billion reduction in their federal income taxes from the Dependent Care Tax Credit (see page 36) in 1983. This is the major form of governmental support for child care, and it has been retained in the 1987 tax law.

Licensing standards and regulations for family day care vary widely from state to state. In 1986, 47 states required some form of licensing or registration, though few specified requirements for providers except their age (usually 18) and the lack of certain criminal convictions. It is almost *too* easy to become a licensed provider.

References

Bureau of the Census. (1983). *Child care arrangements of working mothers: June 1982.* Current Population Reports, Special Studies Series P-23, No. 129. Washington, D.C.

Bureau of Labor Statistics. (1986, March). *Current population survey.* Washington, DC: Author.

PART 1. DECIDING TO START

Is family day care a good job for me?

For some people, taking care of young children is a dream come true. For others it can be a nightmare. Use this self-evaluation to help you think about your personality and situation, and whether you will be likely to succeed as a family day care provider. Continue reading this section after you have completed the self-evaluation.

Factors to consider

Maybe you just know that a career as a family day care provider is right for you. Perhaps you are still unsure. Maybe you need more time to talk to other providers, visit their homes, and think a bit more about it. A good way to try out this kind of work is to assist or substitute in another home. In the process of visiting others, you will learn about your special preferences for how you want to set up your own home.

Many people find it helpful to keep a list of all their questions and concerns over a period of time and then to talk with other providers about them. These questions will help you start your list:

What ages of children will you take?

How many children?

During which hours will you provide care?

What fees will you charge?

Will you take children with special needs?

Which rooms of your house will you use for your program?

Will activities be planned, spontaneous with backup ideas and ready materials, or some combination of the two?

Will you prefer to work alone, or with another caregiver, or as a partner with a neighbor-provider?

How will your family be affected?

While there are many steps in making the decision to start, you can make it with confidence if you carefully consider each step. The experience of other providers is invaluable—if you have doubts, talk to others who are familiar with the details, attend a meeting of providers, and/or attend college or community training classes or conferences.

To find out the names of providers in your community, contact a local child care referral agency if you have one. If not, contact the state or local agency responsible for child care licensing or registration. See the Appendix for a list of groups that may be able to help you identify provider groups near you.

Evaluate your potential

Family day care self-evaluation

This rating task will help you decide whether being a family day care provider would be a good job for you. It looks at many characteristics of successful providers. These characteristics were selected on the basis of conversations with providers and referral agency staff members and on research.

FAMILY DAY CARE SELF-EVALUATION

DIRECTIONS: Think about each trait and how you would rate yourself on it. Then put an X at the place on the line that shows how much you feel you have that trait. For example, if you strongly agree, put an X on the far left. Put your X on the far right if you strongly disagree.

STRONGLY AGREE   MILDLY AGREE   NEUTRAL   MILDLY DISAGREE   STRONGLY DISAGREE

1. I enjoy children very much, and think I could work well with them hour after hour.

2. I am a flexible person who can usually figure a way out of any problem.

3. I have good common sense, and handle emergencies well.

4. I am generally warm and affectionate.

5. I am fairly organized, and able to keep financial records.

6. I do not mind my house being messy sometimes. I can put the children's needs before my housework.

7. I am willing to rearrange the furniture in some rooms of my house to accommodate toys and play equipment.

8. I tend to take life lightly, and have a good sense of humor.

9. I usually appreciate my own accomplishments, even if others do not.

10. I am in good health and have lots of energy.

11. A home child care program is acceptable to each member of my family.

12. I would enjoy talking to parents about their children and our day together.

13. I usually speak up when I have a problem with someone.

14. I accept children as they are, and feel a deep commitment to them and their parents.

15. I am able to guide and discipline children kindly and effectively.

16. I expect to offer family day care for at least 2 years, and I will be able to arrange substitute care when needed.

17. I can handle financially difficult times, or I have financial security to fall back on for a few months while I get started.

HOW TO EVALUATE YOUR RESPONSES: If nearly all of your Xs are on the left side of the page (under *agree*), then you will probably find family day care a very satisfying job. If, on the other hand, many of your Xs are on the right side of the page, you may find that this is not the right job for you. If you have a few *disagrees*, but they are not strong ones, then you might decide that you can make special efforts in those areas.

How do you feel about working mothers?
Many people in our culture believe, deep down, that a mother should stay at home with her young child; a growing number feel that both parents should share child care responsibility. Working parents often feel guilty about leaving their children in another's care. You may find this feeling behind some of the things they say and do. For example, parents may express resentment at the closeness between you and their children.

Ironically, many family day care providers also really believe that mothers should stay home with their young children. In fact, that is why many of them became providers—to stay home with their own child or children. You may find this feeling behind some of the things you say and do, too! For example, you may resent how busy the parents are.

Whether conscious or unconscious, this attitude will interfere in your relationships with working parents. Do you think children younger than a certain age should not be in care? If you do, perhaps you should not take children younger than that, or for more hours than you think they should be in care. You should sort through your values on these issues before you start talking to parents about enrolling their children. Ask yourself how your negative attitudes might affect your work with children or parents. If you are unable to accept and respect their lives and their choices, you may want to select another type of work.

Your family, your home, your neighbors

Your family

Families have different ways of bringing child care into their homes. Sometimes every person in the house is an important member of the home child care family. Marie is assisted by her husband, her children, her grandchildren, and a niece. Sometimes couples run their program together, and are equally involved. Sometimes the children become part of your extended family.

In other families, one person is the provider, and others in the family are not very involved with the program. Often some of the family's rooms are closed off to the child care children, and equipment is stored out of sight after they leave. Christine wants to make a home for her family (husband and teen-aged twins) separate from her child care program, so she puts away most of the children's equipment every night—and she puts *all* of it away on weekends!

Although it is difficult to offer a program in your home if others in your family are not supportive, it can be done *if* careful attention is given, *and* action is taken, to deal with problems when they arise.

Before you decide to begin a home child care program, you should talk frankly with each member of your household about your plans, how their lives will be affected, how they can help and support you, and about what they would like from you in return. Sometimes a provider neglects this important planning step, goes to the effort of starting a program, and then changes her mind because it does not work for her family. *Be sure that everyone in your family will at least try to accept your decision, if not actively support you.*

4

It is also important for you to think about what limits you want to set to keep your work from spilling over too much into your family and personal life. Your spouse or other household members may be concerned about the children's comings and goings, phone calls after hours, clutter, noise, being asked to help with the children or the income tax forms, and you being more tired than you used to be. Your children may be worried about whether you will still have enough time and love for them when they see you caring for other children. (Your spouse might wonder about this, too.)

All family members should have individual private space where their things will not be disturbed by the children in your care. To help you anticipate their feelings, you might think about how you would feel if strangers were going to start sleeping in your bed and using your personal belongings!

Your children

Many people considering family day care as a profession are parents who see this work as a way to be at home with their own children. In this situation it is important to consider other issues that may arise and make plans to deal with them. Starting a program will bring change to your children's lives, just as your starting any new job would. There will be a period of adjustment, feelings to cope with, and perhaps behavioral changes to consider. Not only is it hard to share toys—it is especially hard for young children to share their parents. Your child will see you cuddling other children and paying special attention to them.

The way you present the idea to your children is critical. If you make your decision carefully, and are positive and self-confident, your children are likely to trust you to help them make a smooth transition. They very well may not like the changes right away, and may express negative feelings about them. They should not feel pressured to give approval or to make decisions that they are not capable of making. Here are some specific points to think about:

Developmental stages: Consider the specific ages and developmental needs of your own children, and how your work with other children will relate to what they are already experiencing. If you have a new baby, you may want to wait until the baby is settled and you know her or his routines before you introduce new ones. A 2-year-old who is not ready to share toys will do better if there are plenty of duplicate toys. A 4-year-old intent on self-fulfillment may not like the new rules, and will need well-timed, careful explanations and reminders. Teen-agers used to roaming freely through the house need to know your expectations for how they should interact with the children in your care.

Sometimes young children are confused about change because they cannot understand it. They might think that if the other children are going to play with the toys in your house, they will take them home. Or that because they have to share you at some times, they will never have special time alone with you. You can help your own children know what to expect in advance. "I will be taking care of other children, but I am still going to be your mom, Shari, and I will be—no matter what." "The children will come to our house during the day. Then their parents will take them home in the evening. They are not going to live with us."

Communication: Make sure your expectations are known to your children, and your rules and limits are clear. Anticipate any confusing surprises, and discuss them ahead of time. If you visit other providers while they are caring for children, take your own children along so they can see how things work in another home. Listen to what they say to others, to know their concerns and fantasies. Let them express their feelings without worrying about whether

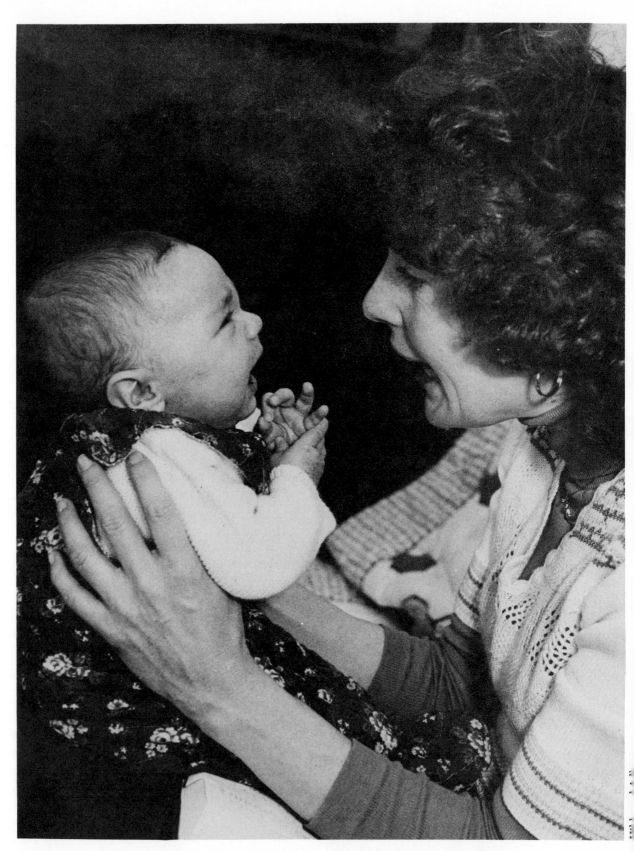

Successful providers like to be around children, and enjoy playing with them.

you will feel guilty or sad or disappointed in them. Remember the reasons why you decided to offer child care, and convey a positive vision of this new step you have chosen for your family.

Feeling special: Sometimes your children will resent it when you are tending to one of the other children. Try to find ways to let your child know that she or he is special to you, while avoiding making the other children feel like second-class citizens. If your child is old enough to understand, you can explain that child care makes it possible for you to stay home — that you have more time together this way than if you worked anyplace else.

Resentment can sometimes be turned into cooperation if you find a special job for your child: welcoming the other children and parents, entertaining the baby while you cook, or passing out the clay.

Practical considerations: Think ahead about problems that will arise. What will you do if your own child becomes ill? What about summer vacations, and other days when school will be closed? How can you assure a family vacation time? What will you do when your child throws a full-blown tantrum in front of new parents?

Most providers find it best to set aside some toys for their own children, and some that belong to everybody. If you rotate toys every so often, your child can set aside a few toys for private use each time. You can explain that your business helps you earn money to buy more toys.

Children are often concerned that your care of other children will crowd them out. Make sure your children have some space of their own, and that they can control who goes there. Involve your children in introducing the home to new children. Let them explain how the bathroom is set up for handwashing, or what the rules are on the stairs. *Establish a daily special time with each of your own children, and be consistent in making sure that it happens.* If during the day your child resents your involvement with other children, you can remind her or him of your special time that is coming, and talk about what you can do together then.

You will find that other providers are an excellent source for helping you understand what your own children are going through and that they are not alone in reacting that way. Let's look at some problems that have confronted providers we know, and how they solved them.

Problems experienced by real providers

1

I started family day care when my daughter was 2½. I did everything I could think of to prepare her. It was a disaster, like a nightmare case of sibling rivalry. She didn't want the kids to come. She was unhappy, and acted out. I was beginning to wonder if I had made a big mistake getting into this.

Talking to other providers really helped. Two-and-one-half probably was not the ideal time to introduce such a big change, but we had done it and I wanted to keep going. By chance, I started making up stories to tell her at bedtime. I made up stories about Shirley and Shirley's mother who did child care. Shirley was pretty mad about the whole child care thing and she had a lot to say about it. Shirley's mother understood, and just listened, and loved Shirley very much no matter what she did. Sometimes Shirley did angry things, and sad things, and worried about things, and said awful things to her mother.

My little girl really got into these stories. She asked for them every night. "Tell me about Shirley — mad." Almost from the beginning her tension eased. Through the stories I was able to give words to her feelings, legitimize them in a safe way, and reassure her. After a while, Shirley started showing a more positive attitude, but I never made her sugary or perfect. It's been 6 months now, and the Shirley story requests are usually crowded out by Little Bear and the Muppets. Things are going great, and my little girl really has fun with the other children and all the activities.

2

My daughter goes to kindergarten with two other children who come to my child care. Every afternoon they would all rush off the bus and race in to see who could be the first to tell me what happened at school. My little girl was always last, and became more and more upset.

I agonized over this one. She really needed me to listen to her after school, but I wanted to be fair and meet the needs of the other children as well. After thinking about it, I realized that this was a time where my daughter had to come first, so I put her first. In a nice way I explained to the other children that I was Kate's mommy and that she needed to be able to tell me about school first. I reminded them that they would get to tell their parents all by themselves, and got them started with their lunch before Kate and I talked. Within a few days we had it worked out. After Kate finishes I listen to the other children. Sometimes I get the same story, but that's OK. I felt that it was important to be there for my own child, and found that I could be there for the other children in a good way, too.

3

My home is very small, and to have enough play space I need to use my son's room for some play and especially for naps. As he got older he began to resent this, and we had some awful scenes about it.

Because we couldn't build on a room for my son to have all to himself, I got creative in thinking about his space. I got the idea of a loft from another provider. We built a loft in my son's room that is totally his space. I put the ladder up during the day so no one else can go there. He takes all his special toys up to his loft. It's so crowded I don't know how he sleeps, but he loves it. Soon we're going to build a shelf for some of the toys. The underneath is welcomed extra space for play. Now that he is older, I also pay him "rent" for the use of his room. It's just a little money, but the principle, and the money, really appeal to him.

4

About when my son turned 3, naptime became a nightmare. I'd been doing child care for several years, but he was at an age when he did not want to nap, and he used that time to get into a power struggle with me. We would argue, sometimes he'd wake the babies, and things would get worse. I was getting angrier and angrier. I tried everything to get him to sleep or just to have a quiet time — nothing worked.

Finally I thought, what would happen if he didn't nap? This was hard for me even to consider, because I really looked forward to those couple hours to put my feet up and get myself together. But I had to try something. He thought it was a great idea. He helped me put the other kids down, and really looked forward to our time alone. We would snuggle up on the couch and watch television or color. I liked it too. Sometimes he gets so comfortable and relaxed he falls asleep! I can't believe how well it worked out.

The issues that come up around our own children are deep and from the heart. It helps to remind ourselves that a moderate amount of manageable stress can be constructive for children, especially if they are allowed to talk about their frustration. They learn to cope with new situations, and are more adaptable in the long run. Family day care can be a fun and happy experience for your own children. It takes thought and practice, but it's worth it.

Your home

Different families also find a variety of ways to set up their homes. Some use all their rooms for the program, others use only certain rooms. Some change their whole house around. Liz cut off the legs of her dining room table so it would be the right size for little chairs — now adults sit on floor pillows. The important thing is to decide how much of the young children's environment you all can live with, and when it is better to make the effort to limit the influence of child care on your personal lives.

Nancy P. Alexander

Try to find ways to let your child know that she or he is special to you, while avoiding making the other children feel like second-class citizens.

You will be much more successful if your space is attractive, large enough, and comfortable. An unfinished basement is not very satisfactory as the only space for children, but it can be perfect for lively or messy activities. This is another aspect of planning you might want to discuss with other providers before you make your decision.

The changes you make are not permanent. If you are flexible and willing to experiment, you can learn what will work for everyone. For a more complete discussion, see the section in Part 4 on Preparing your home, page 45.

Your neighbors

Your first step in making sure your business will be welcomed in your neighborhood is to determine whether there are any pertinent zoning or other restrictions with which you must comply. Perhaps a homeowner's association convenant excludes home child care programs. Make sure you can indeed do this kind of work in your home before you begin to plan your program.

Experienced providers agree that it is important for you to talk with your neighbors before you begin, just as it is important to talk to your family members. Sometimes a provider begins family day care, then later gives up because of neighbors' opposition. Here are some examples of the kinds of problems that may arise:

• Neighbors are generally rude to parents, and ask them not to park in front of their houses or turn around in their driveways.

• You are expected to be the neighborhood babysitter. Neighborhood children drop over whenever you are outside—"What's the problem with watching one more child?"

• Someone, in a conversation about balancing work and family life, asks you what it is like not having a job.

• A group of neighbors meet, without you, to discuss ways to force you to close.

Unfortunately, some people believe that child care should not occur in their neighborhoods. Children's advocacy groups are raising the question of where young children do belong, if not in neighborhoods. Some families have as many children as providers care for! On the other hand, a situation with children shouting in the next yard and extra traffic and parking problems on the street would not be anybody's favorite house next door.

Explain to your neighbors your reasons for wanting to start a home child care program. Tell them what precautions you are taking to ensure that they will not be unduly inconvenienced. Assure them that you want to hear about it if they are being bothered by your business, and that you will make every reasonable effort to resolve problems that come up.

Invite your neighbors to come and see your home soon after you begin. Be thoughtful about putting away yard toys in the evening. Perhaps you have an older neighbor who could become a "foster grandparent" for your program. Sometimes the neighborhood children can be included in your activities. The neighborhood may become a strong support to you, and your community may become closer because your program offers a central focus.

"Why I started a family day care program" — Stories from four providers

1

My first little boy was about 6 months old when I started taking care of a friend's 3-year-old. She was on AFDC so I had to get licensed so I could get reimbursed. Pretty soon I had six 2-year-olds. Then I got down to fewer children when I had my other two. When they got older, I got two sets of twins, and then they had another child, so I became licensed as a group home.

My husband doesn't go to work until 2:30 in the afternoon, so he helps me—we're co-licensed. We've met other couples who do child care together at Association for the Education of Young Children conferences.

I'm not sure how much longer I want to keep doing child care. My son might be going to preschool next year. I might work in a center, or in our public school.

Ruth Booth

2

When I started thinking about opening a family day care program, I saw a lot of parents' heartaches because they could not find care. I wanted to offer quality care. Because we had just moved, I wanted Tisha and Anthony, my children, to be more ad-

10

justed before I started working away from home.

I wondered about how the program would affect my family. Would I want young children all day, 5 days a week? I wondered if the child care children would work into my environment, if my children would get along with them.

If there is a significant other or husband, the provider needs to think about how they'll deal with toys being everywhere, and the diapers. Also how the provider can have time for herself. You could go whacky without other adults. It's important to network, to call other people. Right now my husband is my closest support. Usually I talk to him by phone every day just to keep me going until he gets home in the evening.

Laverne Jackson-Barker

3

I became a child care provider when I became pregnant, to support my basic belief that very young children need to be around their mothers; to explore my lifelong interest in human development; and to fulfill my desire to establish myself as an independent businesswoman.

Joan A. Kauffman

4

Mom raised us kids. I want to raise our kids at home. When Jason was 8 months, a friend needed someone to sit for her two daughters at their house. It was a way of watching Jason and making some money.

After a couple of years we moved, and it was easier for her to drop the girls off at our house. It just snowballed, watching friends' children.

In the meantime, I met Janet (another provider) when I moved here, and she said, "You should get licensed. Stop fooling around." I'd been taking children whenever they showed up, and having different rules for my friends. The children were sick a lot, so I didn't get paid when I had planned on the money.

Before it was haphazard. Being licensed, I've gotten down to business. I've been charging better rates, and going to the Day Care Homes Association, and taking the classes. Now I have so much more to offer the children—I'm always getting new ideas.

Karen Jania

PART 2. PARENTS

"What I want for my child in care" —— Stories from four parents ——

1

Basically I would look for the warmth, of course. I would see what type, if any, activities they had to offer. I would see if I could visit, and bring my child, and see how they would take to each other. The space would be important to me, outdoors as well as indoors. I'd see if they have an area where the children could play, and the toys they had.

For my baby, it depends on how many children they have already. The age group would be important. I'd look for someone my children could play with. I'm not a nut on cleanliness, but I don't like filth. Also I'd look at the type of eating arrangement: Is there a hot lunch? And what type of discipline is there? I'd want to see time-outs, not physical punishment. Physical punishment doesn't work anyway, it just wears you out.

Marlene Atkins

2

When I walk in, I want to sense that it's a loving, warm, open place—cheerful and positive. I want to see that the house is geared for children—set up for them to explore and have fun, and not have to be afraid. I want a person who talks to the children respectfully. I want the person to have the attitude that life is rich, and not to feel like a victim. That person has so much time and influence with my child. I would like there to be an attitude of questioning, encouraging my daughter to question, and to be interested in a variety of things. TV is OK for "Sesame Street," but I don't like much TV viewing. I would rather there be more time for interaction with children, maybe music in the background.

I want there to be loving, touching, hugging, physical contact. Pets are OK, but no smoking. I prefer a place where they don't have their own little children—or else I would need to sense that my daughter would get as much attention as their own children.

Ruth Freedman

3

The most important thing I look for in family day care is a caregiver I feel comfortable leaving my child with; someone who will respect her needs and enjoy her, and who has values similar to mine concerning nurturance and discipline. The second thing I look for is safety. A child-proofed play area, policies that ensure safe field trips, and in general, evidence that the caregiver has anticipated and guarded against the ways my child could be hurt. Thirdly, I look for indications that my child could enjoy her time in this person's care; routines during the day that offer her a chance to vary her play, to encounter new toys or new activities. Finally, I want the caregivers to acknowledge my need to still be in the picture; to offer regular conferences for example, where I could learn about my child's behavior in child care, and we could join together to look for solutions to any continuing problems.

John Reiff

12

4

I'm looking for someone who will respond to my baby. In particular, someone who understands how she asks for things, what it means when she cries. I want to see how the caretaker handles situations, such as a crying baby, a minor fall, spilled juice. Are the kids having a good time? Are they watching TV?

I want Jennifer to have security, to feel good about herself. I want her to have a safe place to play and explore. I want to see some play equipment. I want her to want to learn about her environment.

I want there to be enough adults to take care of the children. I want to feel like I would enjoy spending a lot of time at this place, with this person.

I don't want someone who views child care strictly as a business operation. I want to see that she likes children and cares about what they are getting out of the experience.

Betty Hardee

Your relations with parents

If you decide to become a family day care provider, you will not only be opening your home to children, but to their parents as well. *Developing and maintaining a good working relationship with parents is crucial to the success of your program and to the healthy development of the children and families you serve.*

The child's life must be shared by parent and provider together as partners. You should exchange details about the child's day. To do a good job, you need to know about how children slept the night before, and when they are excited about where they are going after they leave you. Parents should hear about the joys and satisfactions of their children's time with you, not only the frights and frustrations.

When problems arise, as of course they will, it helps if you trust and respect each other, and can talk easily. Examples of potential conflicts that you may need to resolve are:

• finding a mutually agreeable approach to toilet learning
• figuring out how to help a child who is feeling too much pressure from older brothers and sisters
• working with a parent's strong feelings about the child's religious education

There are several ways you can work toward this openness.

• Support each parent by trying to understand each one's situation and perspective. Build a positive relationship with every parent.
• Appreciate each child, and talk with parents about your positive observations of their child.
• Try to check in with each parent every day. Sometimes you will need to discuss topics without the children or other parents present.

Charlene invites parents to stay for a cup of coffee when they drop off their children before 9:30 a.m. A brief evening phone call works well for keeping in touch, if you haven't had a chance to talk or need to discuss a sensitive issue. Write a note if it is easier — notes encourage conversations. Marianne keeps a notebook on the counter for messages and information. Both she and the parents write in it. Kerry has a form that parents take a minute to fill out each morning, so that she does not have to stop an activity each time a parent arrives (see Figure 1).

• Schedule parent conferences at least twice a year so you can discuss perceptions and concerns at leisure. Conferences are important for discussing subjects that do not come up in day-to-day conversation.

Figure 1. Kerry's arrival form

Child's name _____

Time of last meal _____

Sleepy? _____

Any comments:

_____

_____

_____

Five Cs of parent relations

Common sense

Your home child care program is your job, and you are the one who should decide what it will be like. From the beginning, make decisions by asking yourself "What do I want?" "Is this the best thing for my program? For the children?" "How would I really feel if . . . happened?" Think through what is right for you. Then feel confident in your decisions.

You cannot please all the parents all the time. Set realistic expectations for yourself and each parent. Many new caregivers are eager to meet everyone's needs and to impress parents with their wonderfulness. They overcommit themselves, working too many hours or taking too many children. Be careful to avoid the super-provider syndrome. Learn how to say "No," as well as "I'll get back to you. I have to think about it." If you do not know how to handle a situation, you might try thinking of someone you know who would handle it well, and ask yourself what that person might do or say. Then make your own decision and stick with it!

Consistency

You will have to decide how to handle the special needs of each family. Flexibility is good when it is needed, but total inconsistency drives people to madness. When you decide what you want, feel confident in your choice and be consistent. For example, if you have a policy that a child with a temperature higher than 100° F should be taken home, you should be consistent in expecting each parent to come pick up their sick child when called. Do not feel that you need to be swayed by every complaint or request. Think carefully about your rules and expectations and your day's plans. Make your decisions — then explain to parents, firmly but calmly, why you are doing what you are doing.

On the other hand, it is important to really listen to what parents say. Sometimes a parent will be aware of something you do not see, and be able to help you understand. Be open to a good suggestion! Do not be afraid to make a change suggested by a parent when you think it best. The most effective providers are always looking for helpful suggestions, and recognize good ideas when they hear them. They are not afraid to be open, and they are not afraid to stick to what they think is right.

Another form of consistency is important — working parents need consistent child care, and young children need consistent caregivers. You should have one or two reliable substitutes who know the children and your home, who can fill in for you when you are sick, on vacation, or absent for other reasons (see Substitute caregivers, page 29). Likewise, if you are not prepared to make a commitment to care for children for a fairly long time, you probably should rethink your decision. Children do not thrive when they are cared for by a parade of strangers, or when they must adjust to too many broken relationships with important adults in their lives.

Communication

To avoid confusion, communicate your expectations and preferences to parents in writing. Contracts, newsletters, daily logs, notes, and bulletin boards save time, avoid misunderstandings, and let you use your conversation time for less routine matters (see the sample letter to new parents, page 17). Parents often need help in learning to pay attention to written communications.

There are very few problems that cannot be resolved if attention is paid to them by people who respect each other. Sometimes listening to a parent and confirming your support without making judgments or recommendations will make a big difference. Time spent in this way is time gained in the long run. If you find this aspect of caregiving especially difficult, a workshop or course in human relations might be a worthwhile investment for you.

Caring

You will become emotionally involved with the parents if all goes well. Just as you will develop feelings of caring about the children in your program, it will be important for you to cultivate respect and appreciation for their parents. Helene asks parents to walk in without knocking, so they will feel it is their home too. While you do not have to love each one, nor meet every need, you should have an honest concern for each parent's point of view.

Another way providers extend their caring to families is through avoiding the temptation to compete with parents for the

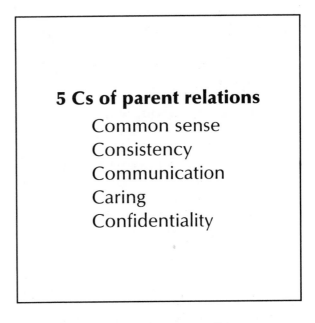

5 Cs of parent relations
Common sense
Consistency
Communication
Caring
Confidentiality

children's love. While you will be very important in the children's lives, you cannot be a substitute for their parents. It may help to view yourself as a support system for families. At times, you may feel you do not get full credit for how much you help the children grow. Many parents feel guilty about "giving up" their child to another caregiver. It is important for providers to come to terms with these realities, so that they can act in ways that are best for children, families, and themselves.

Confidentiality

While caring for young children, you will be in very close touch with their families. You will become familiar with their joys, their issues, and their problems—the ups and downs of their lives. It is your professional responsibility to keep what you know confidential. You must resist the urge to discuss a child or family with others. This confidentiality is critical to building trust in your relationships with parents.

Some providers develop friendships with parents. This can be rewarding for all, but it is important that the provider not try to be therapist or social worker for a parent. If families need special help, you can refer them to appropriate community services.

Procedures for enrolling new families

When you are talking with parents looking for child care, it is important to have a two-way interview: (1) The parent must decide whether you and your home are right for the child. (2) You must decide whether this parent is someone you can work with, and whether your home will be a good place for the child. The match is important — take the time to discuss any concerns on either side.

To decide whether to enroll a new family, a three-step process should be followed: a phone call to discuss basic information such as hours; a visit of parent(s) and child while the other children are there; and a final conversation to discuss and sign the contract.

1. The first phone call

"Uh, hello? Uh, . . . , uhm. . . ." Before you expect your first call from a parent, think through the information you want parents to know and what you need to find out from them. This is a good time to screen out people whose needs do not match your program. You should also consider the style in which you want to communicate. This first impression is important.

The details are specific to you, but some basic information should be discussed in the first phone call. Make a form with space to record what you need to find out and keep a list of what the parent needs to know. Keep these by the phone. **Information you will need from the parent includes:**

- age of child
- hours and days when care is needed
- names and phone numbers of family members
- any special requirements: allergies, disabilities, second language

Parents will need:

- a brief description of the kind of program you have, and the other children who are in your care
- your location, fees, and hours of operation

Be ready to give the phone numbers of your local child care referral service and some other providers who might be able to offer care, if the match is not right with you.

First impressions have a strong influence. Will you sound organized, confident, relaxed? Or will you sound confused or nervous? If you are concerned about this, you can practice. Get a friend or family member to role play a parent on the telephone.

Help your family members learn to take phone messages in a pleasant and business-like manner and to get the information you need to return the call. Attention to such details will distinguish you as a professional.

There might be times of the day, for example while you are serving lunch or putting children down to naps, when you do not want to receive phone calls. You might get an answering machine although it should not be used for long periods, in case a parent needs to get a message to you. You can explain to parents that you think it best not to be interrupted at certain times because the children need your undivided attention.

If the parent's needs match what you want to offer, you can set up a time to visit.

2. The visit

It is important that one or both prospective parents visit with their child for an hour or so, at a time when the other chil-

16

Figure 2. Sample letter to new parents

Dear Parents,

This information sheet about my family day care program is a companion to the formal contract attached. It outlines policies and provides some basic facts to assist you in making your decision about care for your child.

Qualifications. I graduated from Hillside High School and have taken several child care courses at MacKenzie Community College. For the past 3 years, I have been caring for four children ranging in age from 1 to 5 years in age. I am a member of the local Child Care Homes Association and the local affiliate of the National Association for the Education of Young Children. These groups offer regular workshops and information that help me plan for the children and families I work with.

My family. My family is proud that I provide family day care. My husband, John, is a high school teacher. We have two children: Hannah is 4 years old and Chelsea is 16 and a junior at Roosevelt High School. We also have a small dog named Grapes.

Program. I offer child care between the hours of 7:30 a.m. and 6:00 p.m. to give parents time to drive to and from work. Our small, family-style grouping provides some great nurturing experience for the older children and lots of loving stimulation for the younger ones. Our daily schedule usually goes something like this, so that children know what to expect throughout the day: free play during arrival time, breakfast, planning time with each child, project time, snack, active/outdoor play, storytime, individual activities, lunch, a quiet period or nap, free play, snack, outdoor play, daily review time, and saying goodbye.

Instead of detailed lesson plans, I prefer to use my energy to interact with the children and provide activities that will be of interest and just the right challenge for each of them. Our day is flexible, and we try to talk about important experiences—workers trimming trees on the street, for example, or watching the garden grow each day. The materials the children use are intended to help them learn through hands-on experiences so they can test their own ideas and develop their creativity. We have lots of books, blocks, clay, crayons, puzzles, riding toys, stacking toys, dress-ups, games, musical instruments and tapes, and construction toys.

Discipline. I hesitate to use the term *discipline* because it usually means something adults DO to children. Instead, I work to help each child become self-disciplined by seeing how her or his behavior affects others. We have consistent limits based on common-sense rules appropriate to the age of the child. For example, children younger than 3 are not expected to share, but rather to treat each other gently as they play alongside each other. Children learn to feel good about themselves and others in a secure and manageable environment. Children learn to resolve problems between themselves using words. While it is OK to feel angry and frustrated, hitting or breaking things is not OK. Children are never humiliated, but are given sincere positive comments on their behavior. I treat them as I expect them to treat others—with dignity and respect. Children are given choices that are real. They know they can count on me.

Parents. You are free to visit whenever you like. I keep a loose-leaf notebook on the counter that outlines what we do each day with space in the right column for you to make comments or ask questions.

Food and nutrition. A healthy breakfast (if you choose), two snacks, and lunch are provided for each child. Parents are responsible for special diets or formulas. The children often help prepare our food. We use whole grains, very little sweetener, a variety of protein foods, lots of fresh fruits and vegetables—a tasty, appealing diet. Junk foods are never served. I am part of the federal food program and must meet their nutrition guidelines. Menus are posted. Your suggestions for family favorites are always welcome.

Schedule. My home child care program operates year 'round with these exceptions: We are closed on all federal holidays and for Christmas week. I take a 2-week vacation each summer and give you a 1-month notice of the dates. Parents do not pay if the program is closed or for up to 10 days vacation, if you give me a week's notice. Otherwise, payment is expected whenever we are open, in order to reserve space for your child, even if she or he does not attend. Special arrangements can be made for extended absences. Please give me at least 2 weeks notice when you decide to withdraw your child.

Substitutes. I will be the consistent caregiver for your child. If a substitute is needed, you will be notified in advance so the children can get to know the new person. The Child Care Homes Association includes a network of substitutes, and I also have relied upon community college students in child care courses.

Contracts. I have a written contract with parents outlining some of the information here more formally. Children are enrolled for a 2-week trial period, after which I meet with parents to discuss how well the experience is working for all of us.

I hope this sheet will help you in the hard task of selecting child care. If you have questions or just want to talk more, please call me at _____.

dren are there. The visit should be scheduled at a time of day when you will be able to take some time to talk to them, but they should also have a chance to see you doing what you usually do. Ideally they should see a balance of your program—perhaps some free play time and some planned activity.

You may also have an opportunity to see how the new child will fit into your group. You might notice that there isn't another child close to the new child's age, or the parent might feel that the child needs more space to run around. You will also be able to learn about the parent-child relationship.

Different parents look for different things (see "What I want for my child in care," page 12). Some examples are:

• toys and equipment to keep their child busy and happy
• warm interactions with children
• the style of discipline used
• how the other children seem to be doing
• cleanliness and safety precautions
• individual preferences on almost anything. What do you say about table manners (the right way for one family might not be acceptable for another)? What do you do for early reading activities? How much fun is everybody having? How long does any child go with no attention?

The first visit is the time to show parents your written contract and procedures (see Figure 2, page 17, for a sample letter to new parents). We strongly recommend having policies in writing, as discussed on pages 23 to 32. Such policies pertain to illness, discipline, meals, schedule, naps, toileting, vacations, substitute caregivers, and other special information. Although parents might be surprised by your formality, they will understand that you are running a carefully considered service and business, and you will have made your expectations clear.

The visit is also a time for you to learn about the child—what she or he likes to do, eating and sleeping habits, any important details of the child's life. Ask how the parent expects the child to react to being there. You also have a good chance to observe child and parent together.

3. The contract conversation

If the parent chooses to enroll the child and you agree, you need time for a private and leisurely conversation in the evening by telephone. It is important to go over the key points in your contract—do not just hand it to parents and assume that they will heed every point. After agreeing on the details of the contract, you should plan for the child's enrollment. You might provide parents with a copy of the brochure *So Many Goodbyes* (McCracken, 1986) so they can think about the suggestions for making this important transition in their lives.

Three steps to take when deciding whether to enroll a new family

1. The first phone call
2. The visit
3. The contract conversation

Developing and maintaining a good working relationship with the parents is crucial to the success of your program and to the healthy development of the children and families you serve.

Helping children and parents
say goodbye

The parent(s) and child should come to your home together on the first day and everyone should feel comfortable before the parent leaves. For some children this is a matter of hours; for others it takes days or longer. If at all possible, the parent should leave for just an hour or 2 at first, then increasingly longer times, until the child feels familiar with you, the children, the place, and the routines.

We are only beginning to understand the long-term harm done to young children who go through traumatic separations from their parents. Some children do not show any signs of problems. But separation problems are not always obvious at first; they may show up months or years later — even in adult life. The child needs to feel safe in this new place, and to know that these new people are OK. Time invested in a gentle separation will be paid off many times over.

The fear of abandonment is especially strong for (1) babies who experience what is often called *stranger anxiety*, most common between 5 and 13 months, but not unusual throughout the preschool years; (2) children who speak a language different from the provider, especially when they are just learning to speak; or (3) children who have had a traumatic experience in the past when separated from their parents.

On the other hand, when the child is familiar with the situation, the parent should leave confidently and cheerfully. When the parent feels upset at leaving, the child gets the message that something bad is happening. Although it may be hard to say goodbye, it is all right. Here are some suggestions to make the transition go more smoothly.

• If the child is not used to staying with strangers, parents should plan to visit your home with the child for several, increasingly shorter periods, even if the parent has to take time off from work, or hire a babysitter for the other children in the family. This is most important for younger children, especially babies. Jenny asks parents to stay for a whole day the first time, so that they can feed their children in the new high chair, put their children to sleep in the new beds, and get to know their children's new friends.

• After the child is comfortable with the new people and places, help the parent to leave in a guilt-free way. Usually it works best if the parent arrives, says hello to everyone, settles the child into an activity, then says a cheerful goodbye. Sometimes it is useful for the parent to hand over the child in a symbolic way, by placing the baby in your arms, or putting the older child's hand in yours.

• Parents can give the child a family photograph to look at for reassurance. It should be covered with clear plastic and perhaps mounted on cardboard. Parents might also provide something personal (such as a scarf or key chain) for the child to keep during the day. The child might be asked to choose from two or three things the parent is willing to part with. Some children gain a lot of reassurance from such objects, and usually leave them at home as soon as they have become comfortable in the new setting.

• For all babies, and older children who may appreciate it, ask the parent(s) to make a tape recording of their voices as they

Working parents need consistent child care, and young children need consistent caregivers.

speak to the child, perhaps as they would at bedtime, or to read a story. Let the child choose when to listen to the tape. This will be especially effective at naptime. Suggest to parents that they sound calm and reassuring (not guilty or nervous) on the tape.

• Encourage the parent to trust in the choice of child care and convey confidence to the child: "This is a good place I have chosen for you. You will be OK here." Children pick up on their parents' sadness or guilt at leaving them.

• Allow parent and child to have an uninterrupted goodbye. Save your conversations for another time.

• Find extra time to spend with the new child at the beginning, especially at times of transition from one activity to another. Sometimes new providers worry about spoiling a child. Actually, minutes spent during adjustment are hours saved later — once the child is well-adjusted, extra time will not be needed.

• Calmly reassure the new child that her or his parent will return. How you do this depends on the child's ability to understand. With a baby, you might only be able to use a calming technique the parent has recommended. Each baby is different in what works. A frontpack or backpack allows you to carry a baby with your hands free—sometimes this is all it takes to help the child feel reassured. A crib attachment that vibrates and sounds like a heartbeat works well with some babies

With a 2-year-old, you might repeat, "When Mama goes away, Mama comes back." Then, when the mother arrives, say "See, Mama comes back!" With a 4-year-old, you might talk about what the parent(s) and other family members could be doing at the time, and what the whole family will do later when they are all back together.

• Let the child carry around a bottle or pacifier, as well as any of the familiar objects mentioned before. You can plan to change this behavior, if you want to, after the child feels comfortable in your home. Some children like to bring a toy from home for the group to share as a way to bring their two homes together.

• Do not feel hurt or angry if the child is upset at the separation. It is normal and healthy for young children to react that way. It is nothing against you—the child is just letting you know that you are working with a thinking, feeling human being. Do not think that you should stop the child from having these feelings. Instead you should give her or him support and understanding. "It's hard to say goodbye to Daddy, but it's time for him to go. Do you want to wave from the door or the window?"

Positive distractions are also good once the difficulty has been acknowledged—interesting activities can keep one from dwelling on one's sorrows. Occasionally a child uses the issue of separation to manipulate parents and provider, but that is unusual and you do not have to worry about it at first.

Sometimes no efforts are effective. You may find yourself in the extremely upsetting situation of caring for a child who cries a lot and cannot be consoled. If nothing else can be done, you may need to get some relief from the constant crying. This is not a failure on your part. It is a sign of your professionalism that you know when you need help. Make sure you have a substitute caregiver who can take over for a while so you can regain your composure (see page 29).

When it just doesn't work out

On very rare occasions, a child or parent may not adjust to your particular setting, and you may not be willing or able to change the situation. For this reason it is important to have a trial period, as explained in the section on contracts (page 30). Perhaps you can help the parents find another child care situation that would be better, with fewer children, younger ones or older ones, or whatever seems needed. It is important, if you decide after careful thought that it just isn't working out, that you do not blame the child or parents. Instead, do your best to explain the problem to the parents in objective terms, and to help the family find a more satisfactory solution to their needs.

Reference

McCracken, Janet Brown. (1986). *So many goodbyes*. Washington, DC: NAEYC.

PART 3. FAMILY DAY CARE IS A SMALL BUSINESS

Often the same people who are drawn to working with children are reluctant to be hard-nosed in their business management. They risk being taken advantage of, and running less successful programs than providers who learn the fine art of being kind-hearted but firm in standing up for what they think is best. Home child care is a business—a business that includes caring about the people for whom you are providing services. Toys 'n Things Press calls it "loving for a living."

Many talented people stop working with young children because they cannot afford to continue. We encourage providers to make a decent wage for their important work. We also encourage them to make their work go smoothly by having well-thought-out, consistent policies. You should think about your business as well as your caring. Try to define the boundaries between your emotions and your business —do not hesitate to take a clear-headed approach to business decision making. You will not lose your loving approach if you are businesslike about such things as fees and contracts. You can love the children and do business with their parents, and do both in a caring way. By caring for your own needs as well as the families' needs, you help to ensure that you will have a healthy, stable program.

This chapter outlines good business practice for family day care providers. It begins with suggestions about your policies: fees, hours, trial period, food, infant supplies, emergencies, illness, vacations and holidays, substitute caregivers, naps and rest, discipline, spare clothes, and program. You may want to refer again to the sample letter to parents that outlines many of these policies (see page 17).

Your policies

Fees

The fees you charge will provide the financial base for your business and your income. Setting your fees, explaining them to parents, and collecting them are necessary tasks. To succeed as a business, you must generate an adequate and consistent income.

We encourage providers to charge a decent amount for their labor and expertise. Setting fees involves some difficult decisions. In the past, child care providers have tended to keep their rates low, in sympathy with the financial strain that parents feel. Child care is a labor-intensive and important job, yet parking garage attendants are often paid more to take care of cars.

Another factor that keeps child care fees low is that some people think that caring for children should be done out of the goodness of one's heart rather than for an income. Taking care of children is seen by many people as something that just gets done, usually by women. No other profession is burdened by such expectations. But it is tricky to mix caring and making money. Providers must first and foremost enjoy children and want the best for them. Money should not be the first motivation. On the other hand, there is no reason to feel apologetic about wanting to make a decent wage.

For low-income families, child care expenses can be exorbitant. Recent cuts in governmental programs offering child care support to low-income parents have added to the problem. On the other hand, many middle- and upper-income parents are willing to pay more than they do for child care. The National Day Care Home Study (Administration for Children, Youth and Families, 1981), for instance, found that almost 60% of parents who used family day care were willing to pay more for the services they were receiving!

There are two ways you can charge different rates that take into account parents' income. One way is to offer scholarships. For instance, you could set a rate that is a little higher than you would otherwise use, and offer two scholarships of $25 a week.

Another way is to use a sliding scale fee structure, charging higher-income parents more than low-income parents. If you choose this approach, you can explain to the higher-income parents that they are not paying for the care received by low-income families — they are paying only the true cost of good quality care. The lower level fees are supplemented because you are accepting a lower income. Some providers use last year's income tax form to document parents' income in an effort to be sure they are being fair to all.

Either of these fee structures may be difficult to use if you are just starting and worried about not getting enough children. Unfortunately, it is harder to increase fees by a large amount after people are used to lower rates, so you need to set realistic fees from the very beginning. These factors may help you determine how much to charge, because fee levels vary widely in different regions of the country and within each community:

• Rates for part-time care tend to be slightly higher per hour than rates for full-time care.

• Some providers offer reduced fees for additional children in a family, to children of friends or relatives, or to low-income families.

• Some providers charge about $10–20 per week extra for babies because they require more individual care.

• Some charge on a per-day or per-week basis instead of an hourly rate. Some charge on a scheduled slot basis, where the parent contracts for a weekly rate, and is responsible for payment whether the child attends or not. The idea behind this is that the home is open for business and saving a space for that child. (If you choose to do this, you can explain that your budget is based on full enrollment for each child's space.)

• Often there is a higher rate for late pickup. Chris charges $1 for every 3 minutes after 5:30. She hardly ever has a parent arrive later than 5:30!

In setting your fees, consider the quality of care and convenience of what you are going to offer, and how that compares with other providers in your area and the rates they charge. Some parents will happily pay more if you:

• care for just a few children,
• have especially nice toys and equipment attractively arranged,
• have good training or experience,
• have a good location, or
• simply because they feel you will be the right person to care for their children.

When you have set your fees, you should consider them fixed. Do not allow parents to negotiate for a lower fee. Other professional fees are not negotiable.

You will undoubtedly want and need to raise fees once a year, for instance on September 1. Give parents advance notice, preferably in your contract. You can use the current inflation rate as one indication of how much your costs are going up. Providers often charge less than they would like to when they begin, then gradually increase their fees as their reputations and waiting lists grow.

Whatever your rates are, it is important that you be clear with parents about your policies regarding fee payment.

The freedom and peace of mind you gain from having a good substitute list is worth a lot of effort.

• Specify when fees are due—usually on Monday or Friday, for the coming week or the week that has passed.

• Specify whether you accept checks, cash, or both. Set a policy regarding bad checks and adhere firmly to it.

• Specify your policy for parents' vacations. Christina allows families up to 20 vacation days per year when no fee will be charged.

• Specify how much notice a parent must give before withdrawing (usually 2 to 4 weeks).

• Do not overlook late payment. That is poor business practice—if you allow parents to fall behind in their payments, you risk them leaving without paying you what is due.

• Do not hesitate, in cases of extremely overdue payment, to tell parents that it is your policy to go to small claims court to recover unpaid fees.

Your policy for collecting fees might include the following steps:

1. Two days before payment is due, give all parents written bills.

2. On the first day that payment is late, give those parents a written statement specifying the amount due, the period covered, and the date that the payment was due.

3. If they cannot pay immediately, you can agree upon when payment will be due, and specify that in writing. Remind them the day before that date.

4. As soon as you suspect that there might be trouble, notify your local credit bureau of the amount of the debt, and the date it was due, with a carbon copy to the parents. Call the credit bureau to follow up.

5. Discontinue child care for that family and go to small claims court.

Make sure that parents get this policy in writing when they enroll. If you spell out your policies along these lines, parents will know that you are serious about your business. Then, if you have to resort to such measures as notifying the credit bureau, they will know that there is nothing personal—you are simply following policy.

Of course this business approach must be balanced with genuine caring for the family. You might decide to accept their hardship knowing that you may never get paid. You may be convinced that it is essential for the child to stay in your care.

Hours

Parents' child care schedule needs vary greatly, depending on the length of their work day and their commute. Some work weekends or part-time, some work rotating shifts. Others have irregular hours and need drop-in care. There is no one right time for you to be open. Here again, you should think about what might work best for you and your family.

In some families it is best to limit firmly the hours you offer child care; in others the hours can be very flexible. Karen emphasizes that she is strict about her 5:30 closing time during her first conversation with parents. Liz takes children any time, day or night, 7 days a week.

Trial period

As discussed in the section on enrolling new families (page 16), you should talk carefully with new parents about whether there is a good match between what they want and what you offer. But regardless of how careful you are in taking new families, it is possible that a family will not be right for your home, or your home will not be right for that child. You cannot always anticipate everything ahead of time. For example, you may find out that the mother has strong opinions about what you should

be doing, and they clash with yours. Or the parent never pays your fees when they are due. Or you have no other children close to the child's temperament, and you realize the child will never be happy in your home.

Most providers feel they know if the match is satisfactory after 2 weeks, so that can be designated as a trial period. Occasionally it is wise to ask a family to find other care, rather than to stick it out in an unworkable situation.

Sometimes a child is hard to live with, or has difficulties that require regular work with a specialist, but there is no preferable or affordable alternative child care. In those cases we strongly urge providers to seek help from social services in the community. If no organization is able to provide the help, you might be able to get an agency such as resource and referral to support providers to do the important work of caring for a child who might otherwise get shuffled around in an unsatisfactory way.

If you find that you must ask a family to leave, usually it is best to sit down and explain the situation simply, honestly, directly, and without guilt. For example, "He would do better in a child care center or nursery school where they offer lots of activities for children his age." Ideally, you do not want either child or parent to feel kicked out of your home. Instead you want to help them find a better situation.

Food

You should specify to parents what kind of snacks and meals you will provide, at about what times of day. Inform them of anything special in your nutrition program —tell them if you serve real fruit juices, or do not serve sweets. Most parents will be thrilled to find a caregiver who is so thoughtful about children's nutrition. Sometimes parents request special nutritional considerations for their child (such as no sugar, or no milk products). Again, decide what will work for you. Perhaps the

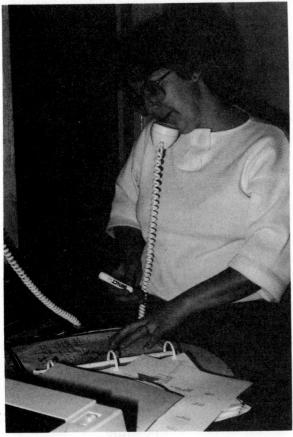

Experienced providers agree: Getting licensed, and claiming tax deductions for your small business, reflects an attitude that child care is a profession.

parent will need to supply special meals if you cannot accommodate the request, such as for a vegetarian diet.

If you are licensed or registered, you are eligible for a substantial reimbursement for your child care food expenses (see Child Care Food Program in the Appendix).

Infant supplies

Specify whether you will provide diapers, formula, and baby food, or whether parents should bring these. It can be a nuisance to remind parents to bring supplies; many providers simply charge more for babies to cover the extra supplies and time required. If a mother is still nursing her baby, perhaps she can arrange to come to your home for a midday feeding. Marie keeps her living room as a quiet place just for two nursing mothers. Many states have strict rules in their licensing or registration guidelines for infant feeding and diaper changing. Be sure to be clear about what types of diapers you can accommodate and any other policies specific to infants. Some new parents may appreciate guidance about introducing appropriate solid foods for their infants.

Emergencies

In most states, you will receive emergency cards for each family when you go through the licensing or registration process. If you do not get these cards, you can draw up your own emergency form for parent signatures. It should legally authorize you (and any substitutes whom you will be leaving alone with the children) to seek emergency treatment for the named child if the parent is not present. Some providers get the signatures notarized. Many hospitals will not treat a child who is accompanied by someone other than a parent unless they have such authorization.

Other necessary emergency information includes the child's full name; name, address, and phone number of parent(s) or legal guardian(s); the name and phone number of the child's health care provider and preferred hospital; any allergies or continuing medication; names and telephone numbers of at least two people who could pick up the child if the parent is not reachable; and the names of others who are authorized to pick up the child. You must release the child to a parent unless there is a custody agreement stating otherwise. If one parent has legal custody, you need that parent's authorization to release the child to the other parent.

If you will be taking children on field trips, you should ask parents to sign a permission statement saying you are authorized to transport the child on field trips as part of your child care program—or you can get individual permissions for each trip. Be sure to carry the emergency cards with you whenever you leave your home with the children.

Unless you have a health care background, you will be much better prepared to handle emergencies if you take a first aid and a CPR course from your local Red Cross.

You should have detailed fire evacuation and weather emergency plans for how you would get the children out of every room in your house that they use. If you use the basement, there should be a window exit located far from the stairs.

It is critical to have a back-up caregiver who can come immediately to take care of the other children in case you must take a child to the hospital or handle some other emergency. See the section on substitutes.

If any type of emergency happens in your home, be sure that all parents are given accurate information about what happened, what you did, and what the outcome was. Take the time to write down the details as soon after the event as possible.

Illness

Specify your procedures for children who become sick during the day, or arrive sick. State laws usually require that a contagious child be isolated. Some providers will care for a child who is not very sick if the child is content to stay in a room away from the other children. Insist that parents plan for emergency backup care if they may be unable to leave work.

Sometimes providers' own children get sick. You should have a plan that allows you to continue to offer child care, knowing that your own child will be well cared for. Be sure you have contingency plans if other family members should contract a contagious disease, or if you should become ill.

Ask the parent to specify in writing the exact dosage of any medication to be administered, and time it should be given. In most states you must have written permission to give any medication to a child. You may want to include permission in your contract to give an aspirin-free pain reliever.

Health questions can usually be answered by a public health nurse at your local county health department. Some providers find a pediatrician or pediatric nurse who is willing to answer their questions without charge.

Providers and parents often wonder how to determine when a child is too sick to stay in a home child care program. It is best to work out your policies with a health care professional and your health department. You will also find guidelines in *Healthy Young Children: A Manual for Programs* (Kendrick, 1987). Some providers keep slightly ill children under certain conditions. Generally, children who feel miserable are more comfortable in their own home with a member of their family. We urge providers to keep this in mind, and to encourage a parent to stay home with the sick child whenever possible.

Vacations and holidays

Give ample notice before you close for vacations and holidays. Parents who count on you for child care need to know what to expect so that they can make other arrangements. One of the most common reasons parents withdraw from a home child care program is that it was not open when it was scheduled to be. If parents need care at a time when you want to be away, it is usually better to hire a substitute than to close. Even if holidays and your vacation plans are specified in your contract, it is a good idea to remind parents two weeks in advance about when you will be closed.

If you decide to allow families some vacation days when no fee will be charged, be sure to specify in your contract how many days will be allowed.

Substitute caregivers

In the past, when a babysitter was mildly ill, she usually cared for children anyway. If she was very sick she probably left families desperately struggling at the last minute to make other arrangements. An important aspect of today's professional family day care service is steady care that parents can depend on. Accidents do happen, you will get sick, and you will need some time away from children.

You should find two or more reliable people who can substitute for you when necessary. They should visit your home and get to know the children and routines **before** they have to sub for you. It can be a challenge to find subs who will work for the wages you can afford to pay, whom you trust absolutely with the children, and who are likely to be available at the last minute. But the freedom and peace of mind you gain from having a good sub list is worth a lot of effort.

The growing teacher shortage among child care centers makes finding good subs especially difficult. The next time you raise your fees, you might explain that you need to increase the amount you have budgeted for substitutes so parents can be assured that they will have a reliable caregiver in your absence. Your contract should spell out your policy on the use of substitutes, and parents should be given the name and telephone number of any sub, preferably in advance.

Subs should be given a tour of your home to learn where supplies and toys are kept. This information should be given in writing and discussed:

1. Emergency procedures (including fire, poisoning, injury, choking), and address and phone number of an emergency back-up person. Some providers ask parents who are nearby to serve as an emergency back-up. Post emergency numbers next to your telephone, including your own address and telephone number (it may be easier to read than think in an emergency).

2. Location of and information on the children's emergency cards (see page 27)

3. Daily schedule

4. Basic rules for getting along together and using equipment

5. Special needs of individual children (such as allergies, toileting, behavior problems)

6. Health procedures (such as washing dishes, cleaning the diaper changing table after each use)

7. A list of the children's names and descriptions, and nap, meal, and other procedures

Naps and rest

Include rest time in your daily routine. Everyone benefits from some quiet rest time each day, including you (or maybe especially you!). Decide upon a daily routine for rest time and use it each day. For instance, you could plan half an hour for free play after lunch, get ready for resting, have a group story, and then have 1 to 2 hours of rest or sleep time, depending on the individual children. Each child should rest in the same place every day, not too close to others. Separate those who tend to keep each other awake.

Many providers tell us that children who do not nap at home will readily nap or rest in the child care setting. You can assure amazed parents that peer pressure works in mysterious ways. Most 5-year-olds can learn to enjoy a private rest time if it is a positive experience, even if they have not taken naps for years. The child and parent may benefit greatly from the child being rested when they get home. Also, there is more time for them to be together in the evening.

Discipline

Good parents and caregivers respond to problem behavior in ways that help children learn better methods to control themselves and meet their needs. Good discipline never makes children feel that they are bad or shameful people. Devise a few simple rules that help children respect others while meeting their own needs, and that allow for cooperative, productive play. State rules in positive, simple words. Encourage, appreciate, and respect children's individual abilities.

Discuss your discipline policy with parents before they enroll their children — the potential for disagreements in this area is great. A good parent-provider match includes similar approaches to discipline for the child's home and your program.

Spare clothes

Ask parents to dress children in play clothes that do not have to be worried about. Outdoor clothes should be appropriate for the weather. This is a chronic problem area, so you may also want to state directly that "in winter the child should have a hat, mittens, warm coat, long pants, and boots to wear outside every day."

Specify what should be included in a set of spare clothes that each child keeps at your house (these can be recently outgrown clothes). Ask parents to label children's clothes and all other belongings. Even so, you will need to keep a laundry marking pen and masking tape handy. Another way you can make your life simpler is to have extra sets of spare clothes available. Good sources of clothes are families with slightly older children, or garage sales.

Program

Parents should be informed about what their children will do at your house. Will you go outdoors every day, weather permitting? Will you cook together? Will you play with the babies? What kinds of music will you hear and make? Will you teach self-care skills such as dressing for outdoors and tying shoes? Your parent materials should include a brief description of your program (see Part 4).

Your contracts with parents

When it comes to making contracts with parents, it is important for you to think of your family day care program as a business. Future misunderstandings can be minimized if you spell out clearly the details of your service. Put your rules in writing, and include what you will do if any terms of the contract are not followed by parents. In a two-parent family, both parents should sign the contract, so that in the case of their separation they are both responsible for the fees agreed upon.

You may feel uncomfortable the first few times you ask a parent to read and sign a contract. Home child care programs have not always been seen as such serious business — you will be a pioneer of sorts if you are so professional. Parents usually appreciate this approach, because it indicates to them that you plan ahead, pay attention to details, and probably will give similar attention to caring for their child.

Sometimes it is hard for new providers to know exactly what to specify in their contracts and other policies. Although it is difficult to attend to so many business details when starting your program, it simplifies things in the long run, and avoids many misunderstandings. As a new provider, you might write a contract that covers the first 3 months, with the understanding that you may modify it after that time.

Contracts do not have to be written in legal language to be binding. Just use your own clear language. You may want to write a parent handbook also, to give information

 Marietta Lynch

Childproof every room where the children will be. Imagine any possible accident, and prevent it.

that is not part of the legal agreement with parents. Each home is different, so you should think about what is right for you and your family.

As with all written materials, remember to revise your contract periodically to reflect changes you need to make in your policies. The items included in the sample contract (Figure 3) will give you some ideas in making up your own contract.

Figure 3. Sample family day care contract

Family Day Care Agreement

I/we am/are contracting with (provider's name) for child care. The terms of our agreement are as follows:

Calendar: Please initial your choice of calendar plans.
_____ 11 months (August 1 through June 30), and July as arranged
_____ 9½ months (September 1 through June 15)

Rates:
- $85 per week for full-time child care (7 or more hours per day). Daily rates are available only by special arrangement.
- $2.25 per hour for regular part-time child care with a minimum of 4 hours per day.
- $2.75 per hour for drop-in child care if space is available.
- Weekday overnight care (Sunday through Thursday) is $12 per night by special arrangement. Weekend care (Friday night through Sunday afternoon) is $35 per 24-hour period or $70 for the 2 days. Weekend care is available only by special arrangement.
- Late fee: $5, plus the hourly rate beginning at 5:30 for any child not picked up by 6 p.m.
- Family discount: There is a $2 per day reduction in child care fees for the second child in each family if one child attends full days.

Fees are payable in advance and are due not later than drop-off time at the beginning of each week. Fees may be paid either:
_____ weekly _____ biweekly _____ monthly
Please initial your choice of payment plans.

Hours: The program operates from 7 a.m. to 5:30 p.m., Monday through Friday. Arrival time is between 7 and 9 a.m., and departure is between 4:00 and 5:30 p.m. The late fee is charged after that time. Overnight and/or weekend care is available by special arrangement only.

Food: All food will be provided by the provider at no additional cost. This will include breakfast, lunch, and two snacks. Supper will be provided for children staying late or overnight. All meals will meet the guidelines of the Child Care Food Program.

Payment policies: Two weeks written notice must be given by the appropriate party for any of the following:
1. termination of the agreement by either party
2. increases in child care fees
3. vacation periods for (provider)

I acknowledge that the rates stated here are payable in full for the calendar period chosen above including holidays, children's absence because of illness, and my family's vacations.

Holidays are Martin Luther King Jr.'s Birthday, Memorial Day, Fourth of July, Labor Day, Thanksgiving, and the day after Thanksgiving. I also acknowledge that there will be no child care from Christmas Day through New Year's Day.

Child care is available during July, but I acknowledge that I must request vacation time by May 1, or I am responsible for payment of full child care fees for the month of July. If my request for July care is in by May 1, I pay only for the child care used in July.

I acknowledge that no fee is due when (provider) does not provide child care because of illness or vacation.

I acknowledge that in case of an emergency, (provider) has my permission to make temporary arrangements for my child's care.

Medication permission: In case of a fever during child care hours, (provider) has my permission to administer an aspirin-free pain reliever to relieve my child while I am being notified. (Provider) also has my permission to administer other medication to my child on my verbal instructions given either in person or over the phone.

I acknowledge that my child care fee for (child's name) will be _____ per week for _____ hours of care between _____ a.m./p.m. and _____ a.m./p.m. This fee is payable in advance on the payment plan chosen here for the calendar selected, unless a replacement child fills my child's place should my child be withdrawn.

Child's full name _____

Parent's signature(s) _____

_____

Provider's signature _____

Date _____

Adapted from a form copyrighted by Helene Mayleben.

The licensing/registration
process

What is family day care licensing/registration?

In most states, any person who is paid to take care of a nonrelated child in the caregiver's home, for more than a certain time period, is required by law to become registered or licensed. To become licensed or registered, your house and equipment must meet specific health and safety guidelines set by your state. In most states, you must keep certain adult:child ratios, pass a TB test and health exam, and meet a few other requirements as well.

These regulations vary widely by state. To find out about your state's policies, call your local department of social services or county health department. (If you do not know who to contact, you can call a local child care center and ask for the name and telephone number of their licensing agency.)

A **family day care program** is typically licensed or registered for up to six children, including the provider's own children under age 7. Usually if your spouse or another adult is assisting, you do not count your own children. Often the number of children younger than 12 or 24 months is limited.

A **group child care home** is typically approved for up to 12 children. There must be a second caregiver any time there are more children present than the number specified for a family day care home. Additional fire, safety, and sanitation requirements must often be met. Group homes also are usually limited in the number of children younger than 12 or 24 months per caregiver.

For the sake of simplicity, we will use the word *license* to refer to both the family and group home registration or license.

Should I become licensed?

When people first consider starting a home child care program, they often assume that it is better not to get licensed — licensing seems like a hassle, perhaps an invasion of privacy. They fear that doing things legally means paying income taxes, which would reduce their already too low earnings. They do not want to bother with keeping records. Cheri said she didn't want to run a business, she just wanted to get paid for watching a couple of other children.

NAEYC, in its position statement supporting family child care licensing or registration, maintains that regulation is the best way to fulfill "the public responsibility to maintain healthy, safe, and developmentally appropriate conditions for children during the time they spend in child care. Regulation is a form of consumer protection for parents and personal protection for children" (1984, p. 1).

Experienced providers agree: Getting licensed, and claiming tax deductions for your small business, reflects an attitude that child care is a profession.

Reasons for licensing
There are several legal reasons why people who take care of other children in their homes should be licensed or registered:

- It may be illegal not to.
- A provider who operates without a license faces much greater risk if any kind of

problem comes up (such as a lawsuit, a complaint about child abuse or neglect, or a complaint about violation of one of the provisions of the laws regulating family day care or city zoning).

• Many parents would rather place their child in a licensed home, because they know this means the home has met minimum requirements.

• Business expense deductions for family day care cannot be taken from income before taxes unless the provider is licensed.

• Most referral agencies will tell parents about only those homes that are licensed.

• The Child Care Food Program reimburses some food expenses for each full-time child in licensed homes only (see National Organizations in the Appendix).

• Most insurance agencies require you to be licensed before they will insure your program (see Insurance, page 37).

• It is easier for parents to accept your rules if they know you are following licensing guidelines.

Because much of family day care is still unlicensed, most licensing staff members are eager for you to participate, and are very helpful in suggesting how you might make any changes needed to meet local standards. We urge you to contact your local licensing representative as soon as you decide to start a program to ensure that it gets off to a good start.

Zoning

One of the first things you should do, if you are considering opening a family day care program, is to check the zoning regulations that apply in your area, both with local governments and with any property owners or homeowners' associations. Make sure this type of child care is permitted where you live, and find out if there are any restrictions. There may be a local child care advocacy group or professional association that can answer your questions and help you with any zoning problems. Some property deeds contain restrictions, and some apartment leases forbid operating a small business from your home. Check these too, before you invest a lot of time and energy in preparations.

Taxes

Your income taxes

When you are paid to take care of children in your home on a regular basis, you operate a small business. Therefore you are legally required to file tax forms, whether you operate at a profit or at a loss. You must file both federal and state returns, and in most states you must be licensed or registered to claim any business deductions.

Each year, you will use the basic 1040 Individual Tax Return, that like all the other forms discussed here can be obtained from the Internal Revenue Service (IRS). Your local library may have forms and the instructions for completing them.

The basic form for reporting your business income and expenses (assuming that your business is not a corporation or a partnership) is **Schedule C of Form 1040.** Good recordkeeping of both income and expenses is essential in order to report the proper information on these tax forms.

Income

Keep a journal listing all the money you are paid for child care, whether in cash or check. This log should record the person who paid you, the date of receipt, the period covered by the payment, and the amount.

This amount should then be deposited into your bank account. Cash needed for day-to-day operations should be taken out of the account by check. If you use any cash directly for personal purposes you will have extra bookkeeping work and it will be easier to omit the amount from your records.

Expenses

Your business expenses are all the payments you make, whether by cash or check, for your child care program. Always save your receipts, especially when you spend cash.

You will probably not need a separate checking account unless you use a large number of checks. Your personal checking or savings account should be adequate. Just note which checks you wrote for business purposes.

The better your records, the easier it will be to complete your tax forms at the end of the year. Expenses for typical items such as those listed here may qualify for a tax deduction IF these purchases were made solely for your program.

- toys and activity supplies
- food for the children in your care
- playground equipment
- wages for assistants or substitutes
- advertising
- legal and professional services for your business
- office and recordkeeping supplies
- insurance for your business
- child care related travel (at $0.21 per mile)

Expenses that benefit both your program and your family will not ordinarily qualify as a tax deduction.

Tax regulations also permit you to write off any specific area of your home that is used strictly for business purposes. However, if you own your own home and claim a business deduction, you may not be able to defer the gain from the sale of your home on the portion used for your business. Check with your tax specialist before you decide to claim this deduction. Also, as of 1987, a home office deduction may not contribute to a loss claimed on Schedule C after all other expenditures are accounted for.

These are some other forms that you may need to comply with federal tax regulations.

Schedule SE—Social Security or Self-Employment Tax. This form computes the amount of Social Security tax that must be paid on the net profit of your business. The 1987 rate was 12.31% on earnings up to $43,800. No self-employment tax is applicable if the net profit of the business is less than $400.

Form 4562—Depreciation. Use this form to record the annual depreciation of capital expenditures related to your business. All equipment, including toys and play equipment expected to have a useful life of at least 1 year, should be considered for depreciation. Again, you may need to consult with a tax specialist regarding the proper categories.

Form W-2—Wage Statement. A W-2 should be completed for individuals who perform services for your child care program. These are issued both to the workers and to the IRS each year. Form 941, or quarterly returns, are also prepared for these workers.

Form 1040 ES—Federal Estimated Tax Payments and State Estimated Tax Payments. If you owe more than $500 in taxes from your business, you must report quarterly. Likewise, state estimates may also be necessary if the federal estimated payment guidelines apply to you.

Keeping your records so that you can file your tax forms accurately requires advance planning. Your business plan must include a format for financial recordkeeping, and you may want to consult with a tax advisor before you begin caring for children. Do not wait until the end of the year to try to assemble all the information you will need to file your tax forms.

For detailed information on taxes, a good resource is the two-part series on Business Ideas for Family Day Care Providers: *Basic Guide to Recordkeeping* and *Taxes and Annual Update for Preparing Federal Income Tax Returns*. This series is published by Toys 'n Things Press, Resources for Child Caring, 906 North Dale Street, St. Paul, MN 55103.

The Dependent Care Tax Credit

Working parents, parents actively looking for work, student parents, and some AFDC recipients may be eligible for a tax credit for a percentage of their child care fees. The Child Care Law Center's booklet, *The Child Care Tax Credit*, provides a detailed explanation of the many facets of this credit.

Federal income tax forms that may be needed

- 1040 Individual Tax Return
- Schedule C of Form 1040, Profit or (Loss) from Business or Profession
- Schedule SE — Social Security or Self-Employment Tax
- Form 4562 — Depreciation
- Form W-2 — Wage Statement
- Form 1040 ES — Federal Estimated Tax Payments

Budgets

Some providers follow a strict budget, divided into categories such as food, household supplies, play materials, and equipment. For example, they know exactly how much they have to spend for toys each year — if they decide to buy a toy that costs more than their play materials budget allows, they borrow from another budget category where they will underspend.

Others have no idea exactly how much they spend each year on each budget category, but they have an intuitive sense of their overall budget. They know how much they can afford to spend and stay within the guidelines or they go out of business.

It is wise — if you do not want to risk losing money — to follow a budget closely at first. Even if you change your plans about what you will spend, you have more financial security if you know where you are going to cut (or increase income) to make up for unexpected expenses. After your business is operating with greater financial security, you can reduce your financial planning, if you like, simply by keeping track of your monthly expenses, and comparing them to your average month's expenses.

Figure 4. Sample budgets

These two sample budgets will help you know what you might expect if you become a family day care provider. The first column is from a small program; the second column is from a large group home. Expenses do not include provider's income or fringe benefits.

Income

	Small program	Large program
Fees (includes reimbursements)	$7,780	$29,039
Child Care Food Program	1,909	2,955
Other income	35	60
TOTAL	$9,724	$32,054

Expenses

Food	$1,834	$2,470
Supplies		
Children's toys and materials	192	1,159
Office supplies, copying, computer equipment/ programs	178	2,781
Postage	—	61
Household supplies	98	155
Miscellaneous	—	255
Equipment	—	1,622
Maintenance and repairs	66	613
Wages		
Assistants	—	3,694
Substitute caregivers	76	—
Custodial	—	7,000
Staff benefits	—	*
Tax accountant	—	829
Child care portion of rent or mortgage and taxes	—	9,385
Child care portion of utilities	—	1,551
Insurance		
Liability**	125	159
Accident	50	60
Motor vehicle, if applicable	—	746
Advertising and public relations	—	413
Business entertaining and gifts	62	131
Mileage expenses (20.5¢ per mile)	—	155
Dues and publications	25	74
Conferences	38	88
	$2,744	$33,401***

* Sick and vacation days paid after 1 year of employment; retirement paid after 3 years of employment

** Liability rates may not reflect current premiums (see Insurance, page 37).

*** Because expenses are higher than income for this family day care program, the providers' only income consists of their substantial tax savings resulting from the business expenses that can be written off their income before taxes.

Insurance

Several types of insurance are available for family day care providers. Liability and accident insurance are considered essential. Coverage, availability, rates, and rules vary from state to state.

Liability

Almost every state requires that people paid to take care of children in their homes follow certain health and safety guidelines. Providers are responsible for the supervision of children in care at all times, and for the appropriate handling of any emergency.

The provider is liable, and can be sued in court, if a parent alleges that an accident occurred because of negligence, or failure to exercise reasonable care. You, your employee, and/or your home or property can be found to be negligent. Seven states require that providers carry liability insurance, at least in some situations, and many others strongly advise it.

To find out about your state, call the local office that licenses or registers family day care, or a providers' organization.

Negligence is a legal term that means a person who was under legal obligation to act with reasonable care did not do so. Negligence might take the form of inadequate supervision—for example, when a jury finds that the provider (or assistant) was not properly supervising a child when an accident occurred. Another example is when one child hurts another and a jury agrees that the children were not being adequately supervised. Another form of negligence is faulty maintenance, such as when a swing chain breaks because it is in poor condition, or when icy steps cause someone to fall.

Liability insurance for providers has become expensive and sometimes hard to find (see the Insurance Crisis section that follows). Policies vary. You should read a policy carefully to see what is covered and what is excluded. Ask about any terms you do not understand. Most general liability policies cover four basic types of costs

- bodily or personal injury
- damage to others' property
- immediate medical relief at the time of an accident
- the legal costs to defend you in a lawsuit

Other areas for possible coverage are

- transporting children
- accidents where no one is at fault
- defense costs in the event of physical and/or sexual abuse charges
- damage to your property

There are two basic types of commercial liability policies: *claims made* and *occurrence*. With claims-made policies, you are only covered for incidents that are **reported** during the time your policy is in force. Occurrence insurance covers you for incidents that **occur** during the time your policy is in force. Your coverage is much broader, then, with occurrence insurance.

Shop around to see where you can get the coverage you need for the best price. Use only licenced agents or brokers. You may be able to obtain coverage through a special endorsement to your homeowner's policy if you care for only a few children.

There are several ways you can reduce the chances that you will be sued for negligence.

- Childproof every room where the children will be. Imagine any possible accident, and prevent it.
- Take first aid and CPR courses (call your local Red Cross for information).
- Learn to keep an eye on all the children, even when you are paying special attention to one, cooking, or talking on the telephone.
- Keep walkways, stairs, and sidewalks clear.
- Avoid fire hazards.
- Choose your assistants and substitutes carefully (see Substitutes, page 29).
- Develop and follow clear policies about health and safety.
- Encourage parents to visit any time, and give them your written policies.

The insurance crisis

The child care profession has been faced with an insurance crisis during the past few years. Providers have had difficulty obtaining or affording insurance because of four factors:

access—liability policies were cancelled suddenly; many providers could not find coverage at any price

affordability—providers' liability premiums typically increased 300 to 400%, or more

predictability—high quality programs that had never filed an insurance claim were suddenly unable to renew their policies

coverage—insurance companies that still insure child care homes added restrictions about who is eligible and what is covered. Usually there is no protection from accusations of child abuse or sexual molestation (*Young Children*, 1985).

Because it is so difficult and expensive to obtain liability coverage, it is tempting not to do so. You may be absolutely sure that no abuse will occur, and believe you can offer a safe program that will not have liability difficulties. But the number of lawsuits against providers is increasing, and sometimes there is no truth to the accusations. Even the best providers and programs may be accused of negligence or abuse. You must protect yourself.

A few states have solved these insurance problems satisfactorily, thanks to the active intervention of the state insurance commissioners (Modigliani, 1986). A few have Market Assistance Plans to help providers find the best policy. In most states, liability insurance may be available but expensive or very expensive — or it may be hard or impossible to find.

If you have trouble obtaining insurance, contact your state's Department of Insurance to see whether a Market Assistance Plan is in effect in your state. Here are some other advocacy steps you can take.

1. Be ready to educate insurance agents about their misperceptions about home-based child care. For instance, many people have heard of child sexual abuse in child care — yet most abuse happens in the *child's home*. Child care often prevents sexual abuse because the child is not left in the care of an abusing family member, or because it gives parents a break from the sometimes stressful work of caring for children.

Let agents know you are a professional, that you are licensed, and that you follow strict health and safety procedures. Give some examples; mention your first aid training. If agents state that child care is a high risk profession to insure, ask for their evidence. No research has shown that child care is high risk; there are a few studies that suggest it is low risk.

2. If you own your home and have homeowner's insurance, you may be able to get a child care home rider added to your liability policy, though in some areas homeowners' insurance is being cancelled if the home is used for child care. If you rent, you may be able to get a rider added to your tenant's liability insurance. This used to be the most common way for providers to carry liability insurance. Explain to your agent you are not operating a nursery school or child care center, but are providing family day care. Ask her or him to waive the "exclusion of business pursuits" clause for your child care home. You might remind the agent that the company would insure a family with this number of children, but families are getting smaller now, and they count on people like you to care for their children.

3. If your community has a family day care providers' association or a child care resource and referral service, they may be the best help. Your local licensing or registration office or your state office of insurance should be able to tell you which companies are currently writing home-based child care policies in your state. If you cannot find local information, call NAEYC's Information Service at 202-232-8777 or 800-424-2460 from 9 a.m. to 4 p.m. Eastern time, or The Children's Foundation at 202-347-3300.

Several national organizations are working on this problem, including NAEYC, the Child Care Action Campaign, the National Association for Family Day Care, Save the Children, the Children's Defense Fund, The Children's Foundation, and The Child Care Law Center (see Appendix for addresses).

4. Be persistent and assertive. Call many agents and document what each one says. If you have trouble, send a summary of your efforts to your state insurance commissioner, one or all of the organizations listed in #3, and to your governmental representatives. Perhaps you can work with other providers in your state or region to get group rates.

5. If you are already caring for children, get the parents involved. Their letters or phone calls to insurance agents and governmental representatives are effective. The *Young Children* article suggests that you make the problem visible in your community by writing letters or editorials for newspapers, speaking on radio or television talk shows, and making presentations at city council and other civic organization meetings. Public awareness of the problem is necessary to encourage insurance companies to come up with voluntary solutions (such as California's Marketing Assistance Plan), or to prompt government to intervene.

Other types of insurance

Accident insurance
For a small cost, you can buy insurance to supplement the family's medical insurance if a child or employee is injured.

Motor vehicle insurance
If you will transport children in your car, make sure you have enough coverage on your motor vehicle insurance (sometimes children's medical costs are included in liability or accident insurance).

Medical and health insurance
If you and any family members are not already covered by other medical insurance, you should consider including this protection for doctor and hospital bills. If you belong to a providers' association, you may be able to get medical insurance through it. Remember, you will be exposed to many more communicable diseases when you work with several children.

Disability
This type of insurance covers you if you are injured and unable to work. Policies vary; usually they cover lost income, and additional bills that accumulate directly related to your disability. Most policies exclude pregnancy or prior illness.

Worker's Compensation
If you hire others, this insurance covers them for on-the-job injuries. It is required in many states.

This list of different types of insurance may be intimidating and sometimes irrelevant to a new provider. The first two types are the essential ones. Others might be added, if relevant, after you feel more established. Decide what coverage you need now, and what you might like to get in the future.

Inform parents of the insurance you carry. If your insurance premiums increase, or you add new coverage, explain this to them when you raise fees.

Recordkeeping

Checking account

Financial recordkeeping is simplified when your child care program has a separate checking account (see the section on taxes, page 34). You do not have to get a business account; a personal checking account is fine. All fees and reimbursement income are entered into it, and all business expenses are paid out of it. For small purchases, when you do not want to bother with check writing and accounting, you can keep a petty cash fund. Save receipts of what you spend to enter into your records.

Expense and income records

Several types of books are available in office supply stores to help you keep records of receipts and disbursements by budget categories. These books are intended for small businesses, and may contain many items you do not use. A device called the *Calendar-Keeper* is especially useful for keeping records for family day care. The *Calendar-Keeper* includes space for keeping attendance and fee payment records, expenses in budget categories, mileage records, and menus.

Two sample pages from Karen Jania's *Calendar-Keeper* are reproduced here as an example of how this system works. Figure 5 shows attendance and fee payment records. Figure 6 shows expenses for the March (entered into the appropriate category columns) and the total expenses for the month. The *Calendar-Keeper* can be ordered from Toys 'n Things Press, Resources for Child Caring, 906 North Dale Street, St. Paul, MN 55103.

If you keep a careful checking account record, and either the *Calendar-Keeper* or another form of income and expense record (and mileage records of your business driving), you will have done most of the backup work required to fill out your income and business tax forms. A good recordkeeping system makes filing taxes manageable to do for yourself, or it gives you an easy way to pass on the information to a tax accountant.

Figure 5. Sample attendance and fee payment records from Karen Jania's *Calendar-Keeper*

This figure represents total payments for child care services. This can be added to other income received from your child care business (such as USDA CCFP reimbursements) to get your total month's income.

OTHER INCOME

Date	Source	Amt.
	CCFP REIMBURSEMENT	194.5
	This Month's Total	
	Balance Carried Forward	
	Year-To-Date Total	

MARCH

S	M	T	W	T	F	S
					1	2
3	4	5	6	7	8	9
10	11	12	13	14	15	16
17	18	19	20	21	22	23
24	25	26	27	28	29	30
31						

Figure 6. Sample expense records from Karen Jania's *Calendar-Keeper*

MARCH EXPENSES   10.7

Date	Purchased From	Check #	Purchase Total	FOOD	HOUSEHLD MAINT ITEMS	SUPPLIES	TOYS & EQUIPMT		
3/3	Farmer Jacks	2066	39 70	39 70					
3/6	Sally Heitz	2074	8 25					8 75	
3/10	Farmer Jacks	2079	37 63	29 99	7 64				
3/13	Top R Us	2083	20 64				20 64		
3/17	Kroger	2090	26 19	25 50	69				
3/1	Falsetts	cash	1 35	1 35					
3/9	marmel Gifts	cash	8 32				8 32		
3/9	"	cash	5 20				5 20		
3/5	China Rest	cash	5 30				5 30		
3/9	Child. Small Pres	cash	6 19			6 19			
3/12	K Mart	2065	18 43			18 43			
3/14	Busters	cash	6 49	6 49					
3/23	Kroger	2103	5 36	5 36					
3/24	Farmer Jacks	2104	28 02	26 44	1 58				
3/26	K-Mart	2109	10 45			6 48	3 97		
3/28	J + M	cash	1 93				1 93		
3/28	J + M	2012	5 02		3 64		1 58		
3/30	"	cash	4 06		3 13	93			
3/31	Farmer Jacks	2116	33 14	29 47	3 67				
3/27	Sally Heitz	2111	8 00					8 00	
3/28	Falsetts	cash	2 98	2 98					
	This Month's Total		280 15	167 94	17 22	34 23	39 06	8 41	16 75
	Balance Carried Forward								
	Year-To-Date Total								

42

Finding children

Marketing

Some providers quickly find as many children as they want to fill their home child care program. Others do not have enough children coming to them unless they market their programs. We do not mean *marketing* in the sense of misrepresenting and overselling your program. You cannot be all things to all people, so decide what kinds of services you want to provide to whom and stick with them.

Most parents choose their child's caregiver from word-of-mouth information. It is not usually effective to take out ads in newspapers or put up signs. Instead, talk to people personally. What works is getting the word out about yourself and your program to people who might have the opportunity to recommend you.

If you have already taken care of children, you may want to get letters of recommendation from their parents. It helps to have an attractive business card with information including your hours, the ages of children you care for, and perhaps a few words about what is special about your qualifications or program. Business cards are an inexpensive investment in your business. When you take the children for a walk in your neighborhood, you might bring along some business cards to pass out to interested people you meet. Ask parents to give cards or fliers to their friends and people at their jobs.

Go to the elementary schools nearby, introduce yourself to the office staff, and give them some cards or fliers. Anyone who works with families may be able to make referrals to you — ministers or rabbis, pediatricians, parenting groups, business or civic organizations. Other successful providers or child care centers in your area may be an excellent source of referrals. Sometimes one provider has a community-wide reputation as the person you call to find home child care. Think creatively about your neighbors and networks.

A most important factor in how easily you find children is how good you and your program are. If parents just love the way you interact with children, and see that their children are happy and thriving at your home, they will tell their friends. Good providers are in high demand almost everywhere.

You are also more likely to draw families if your home is clean, safe, and appealing to children. If parents sense that their children would be bored at your house, they are likely to look elsewhere.

A most important factor in how easily you find children is how good you and your program are.

Another important factor is location. The closer you are to major commuter routes or central areas, the more convenient you are for a large number of parents. However, you can be 10 miles out in the cornfields and attract families if your program is good enough. If you reach out to tell your community about your services, and you have good child care to offer, you will most likely find enough children before long.

Referral agencies. The number of child care referral agencies is growing. If you are licensed or registered, you may be eligible to be listed for referrals by the licensing office and other referral agencies in your community. Check the *National Directory of Child Care Information and Referral Agencies,* available from the California Child Care Resource and Referral Network, 809 Lincoln Way, San Francisco, CA 94122, for the agency nearest you.

Patience pays

In our child care classes, we hear a common story: A new provider is worried she isn't getting children fast enough. She eagerly accepts every family that comes along, regardless of age, hours, or the match between parent and provider. Just a couple of months later she has full enrollment. Now she is overextended and already making plans for how she will be more selective in the future.

If you can possibly afford to be choosy, hold out for children whose ages and hours would work well for you and your group. It is also wise to look for parents with whom you think you will have a satisfactory relationship and share common goals for the child.

References

Administration for Children, Youth and Families. (1981). *Family day care in the United States: Executive summary.* (DHHS Publication No. OHDS 80-30287). Washington, DC: U.S. Department of Health and Human Services; Administration for Children, Youth and Families; Day Care Division.

Kendrick, Abby. (Ed.). (1987). *Healthy young children: A manual for programs.* Washington, DC: NAEYC.

Modigliani, Kathy. (1986). *Summary of results of licensing survey.* Unpublished manuscript, NAEYC, Washington, DC.

National Association for the Education of Young Children. (1984). *NAEYC position statements on child care and family day care regulation.* Washington, DC: NAEYC.

National Association for the Education of Young Children. (1985, November). Public policy report. Liability insurance update. *Young Children, 41* (1), 53–55.

PART 4. YOUR PROGRAM

———— Preparing your home ————

Before you begin caring for children, it is wise to transform your home into a place that is childproof, comfortable, and inviting.

Safety

You will want to feel confident that all areas children will use—indoors and out—are safely childproofed. To check, you might want to crawl around on your hands and knees asking, "What could a child possibly get into here? How might I possibly be able to hurt myself or otherwise cause a problem here!?" Make sure all items children should not use are safely locked away or on high, inaccessible shelves. Precious breakables should also be put away. Poisonous plants should be out of reach. Stairs should be well-lighted and secure under foot. Toys should be stored on shelves to avoid falling lids from toyboxes.

All play materials, furniture, shelving, outdoor equipment—everything that the children come into contact with—should be checked every few days for loose parts or any safety hazard. Broken toys and missing pieces discourage play, and should be fixed, put away, or discarded. A doll with a missing limb could be tenderly cared for, and perhaps bandaged or fitted with a pretend artificial limb during hospital play. If beyond repair, some broken equipment can be dissected to see what is inside before it is thrown away.

Sometimes parents are willing to build and repair equipment to keep costs down. Or, a parent can be given a discounted fee for helping with these tasks. Occasionally one or more parents might be willing to build shelves, a backyard climber, or a child-sized picnic table.

While garage sales are often a source of first-rate toys and equipment at bargain prices, older model cribs and other items may not meet current safety standards.

Equipment and materials

What you will need depends on the ages of children, but this is a list of ideal equipment and materials for a child care home serving a wide age range of children:

• child-sized table and chairs, booster seats, high chairs, an infant seat. Tables can be used for eating and for a variety of children's activities.

• individual cribs, beds, or foam rubber pads covered with plastic that can be stored under your beds. Blankets and sheets for each child. If you use your family's beds, lay the child's bedding on top of the made-up bed.

• diapering area (preferably near a faucet) that can be easily sanitized after each use. Nearby childproof, sanitary storage for used diapers. Step stool for sinks and toilet.

• space—to crawl, toddle, run, climb, and to be alone but in view

• outdoor play space (sand, hard surface for wheeled toys, swings, climber, garden) or a nearby park. A covered porch, garage, or carport is ideal for rainy days.

• art materials, including beautiful junk (such as meat trays, egg cartons, computer paper); washable surfaces for messy activities

• water and sand to scoop and pour in plastic dishpans or a larger trough or water table; old throw rugs or other absorbent floor covering

• large and small, simple and complicated toys, including building materials such as wooden and plastic blocks

• good children's books, and a quiet, cuddly place to read. Paperback books can be covered with clear adhesive plastic to protect and strengthen them.

• games, puzzles, vehicles, dolls — child-powered rather than battery-powered

• make-believe props, clothes, and Halloween costumes for dressing up and pretending

• record player, tape recorder, and/or radio

• a fabric carrier for a young baby, and a backpack carrier for babies who can sit up. Many babies love swings and bouncer chairs.

• for older children, a private place with props and equipment that children can rearrange as they choose. Gretchen's basement has a climber, old tables, blankets, a tumbling mat, and miscellaneous junk. School-aged children also need a place to keep their things from school, and perhaps a place to do homework.

See *Toys: Tools for Learning* for suggestions on specific toys for different age groups (NAEYC, 1986).

Setting up

Your home should be set up so children can play happily with each other and by themselves, and so that children can exercise their growing independence — hanging up their own coats or putting dishes in the dishwasher. Sometimes you will want to join in their play, or suggest ways to extend it or make it more interesting. While you will always closely supervise their play, you can't be with all the children every minute. If there are engaging things for children of different ages and interests to do, you will be able to feed a baby or prepare lunch knowing that the children are safe, busy, and happy.

Basic equipment and materials for family day care

• child-sized table and chairs
• individual sleeping places
• diapering area
• space
• outdoor space
• art materials
• water and sand
• assorted toys and blocks
• children's books
• games, puzzles, vehicles, dolls
• props for pretend play
• music
• baby furniture
• storage area

Your job will be easier if you set up your home to simplify everyday routines . Some problems can be prevented by having selected things where the children can reach them (help-yourself toys, children's spare clothes, water cups), and others where they can't (house plants, TV, older children's projects). If children can take care of some of their own needs, without help, it leaves you free to be doing something else for or with them. Their independence also gives them opportunities to feel competent.

To facilitate good play, toys and materials should be attractively arranged and presented. A toy chest with bits and pieces of all sorts usually invites no play at all. Keep most items on open shelves, so children can readily see what their choices are. Special activities might be placed on a table. Furniture that can be moved easily can be rearranged for different activities and for a change of pace. Children will enjoy cooperating with each other and using their strong muscles to help you move it.

You do not need to spend a lot of money on toys and equipment if you set up your home with creativity and care. Make the most of what you have — your own warmth and enthusiasm will be your best equipment, your pots and pans and utensil drawer (with, of course, only harmless utensils) will be especially popular. Cooking, dressing up, playing games, and exploring the neighborhood can be great fun.

Garage sales and used toy and furniture stores often have good toys or equipment in fine condition. Try books from your public library before you decide to buy unfamiliar ones; you may be able to check out records and pictures too. Some communities are lucky enough to have toy lending libraries or similar resources for teachers and child care providers.

Storage

Adequate storage is especially important for child care providers with limited space. Well-designed storage helps reduce clutter and increases play space. Janet uses her hall linen closet for toys. Marianne lowered the hanger bar in a child's bedroom closet, and built several shelves above it. Ken uses every inch of space under the beds for storage of extra supplies in cardboard paper boxes. Boards and cement blocks make sturdy, inexpensive shelves for preschool and older children. Heavy cardboard cartons and wooden crates from grocery stores can also be used to build storage units. For infants and toddlers, make sure shelves are stable enough that children won't tip them over when they use the furniture to pull themselves up to stand or walk.

It is a good idea to rotate toys and materials. Put away items the children are tired of for a few weeks. Bring them out later, and children will enjoy rediscovering them. You may want to assemble theme idea boxes containing all the materials you need for a specific activity, such as playing store or going on a nature walk. Or you might assemble a rainy day box with everything you need for one special project, or with toys that are best used only occasionally.

Every child should have a special personal storage area, even if it is only a shoe box or an ice cream tub. Label it with the child's name, and perhaps a recognizable symbol. Children at Helene's home each have a special sticker marking their cubbies, lunch boxes, and drinking cups. Each child's special area should be off-limits to the other children. This gives the child a feeling of belonging, and a security in knowing special things can be kept safely.

You, as a business person, also need office space. An efficient way to store your administrative and financial records will save you precious time. LaVerna's first office was the back of her kitchen table and the shelf above it, where she kept the children's emergency cards, a shoe box for her expense receipts, and an accordian folder for business papers. After a year, she got her own file cabinet and desk top.

Your program

In this handbook we have chosen to focus on how to start a home-based child care program. You will have many more questions after you are caring for children. Part of your planning before you begin is to think about your program and activities. Many child care homes have no real program — the children "just play" all day. The same toys are always on the shelves, the same art materials are always available but never presented in any way. Planning is essential to avoid boredom and to increase learning opportunities.

Your program — what you and the chil-

Francis Wardle

Put your planning energy into setting up a rich environment—set the stage for the children to come up with their own play ideas.

dren do day by day—will be basic to your professional success and pleasure. If children are bored, not only are they missing developmental opportunities, but also they have more discipline problems and are fussier. All of you will be happier if you have interesting activities that you look forward to each day.

Planning and scheduling

Some providers like to follow a daily schedule, doing the same activities at approximately the same time every day. Other providers like to be more spontaneous, responding to everyone's moods and the opportunities that come along. If you like tight schedules, you may need to learn to be more flexible, knowing that you can never predict too much of what is going to happen. Young children are spontaneous; they have some of their best moments without any warning. One will start dancing to music, and you will all want to stop everything and dance. Another time there will be an earthworm on the sidewalk, and you will want to stop and watch.

A good provider observes the children for activity ideas. Sometimes these ideas require planning. Sometimes they must be followed at the moment, postponing any other plans. Put your planning energy into setting up a rich environment—set the stage for the children to come up with their own play ideas. Everyday living will provide many of the activities. Learning to put on a jacket, spreading peanut butter on a cracker, playing peek-a-boo with a baby

—these are important activities of life for young children.

At other times children will be ready for your ideas. Ideally you should have a variety of activities ready to go, with necessary materials on hand. You can keep a list of possibilities to choose from when something is needed.

While elaborate lesson plans are not appropriate for young children, some routine, some predictability is needed. If you tend to be spontaneous and do things in a different way every day, you may need to force yourself to do things in a more patterned way. Young children like to know what is coming next. It helps to set up a daily pattern of routines for eating, toileting, and resting. You can build your day around these regular routines, so children gain a dependable sense of what is happening next. Even a toddler has some sense of the flow of the day, some notion of a sequence like the following:

First we play,
  then clean up,
    go to the bathroom or have diapers
    changed, and
      wash our hands,
      then we have snack,
        then we have group activities,
          then we usually go outside,
then we go to the bathroom and wash up
again,
  then we have lunch,
    then we have stories, and bathroom
    again
      then we have naps,
  then we have snack,
    then we play.
      Then parents come.

Tell children a few minutes ahead of time that it will soon be time to change activities so they don't have to stop abruptly. Work out sequences that allow easy transitions from one activity to the next. See what you can do to avoid making children wait.

Watch the children's natural tendencies

to help you plan an effective sequence for the day. If they are full of creativity in the middle of the morning, that is a good time to get out art materials. If they tend to get rowdy after snack, that is the time to go outside. If they are sleepy and cuddly after waking up from their naps, reading stories might be a successful activity. If school-aged children resist structured activities when they arrive, they should be allowed free-play time. If you watch carefully, they may even show you by their play that you could be most useful as a provider of dramatic play props. Take your cues from the children.

You will need to adjust your routines as new children bring different needs and personalities to the group. Each group of children is different. You can plan activities, but make sure you flow with children's natural tendencies rather than oppose them.

A good rule of thumb for planning the day is to alternate
  active and quiet times
    structured and unstructured activities
      together times and private times.

The sample daily schedule in Figure 7 demonstrates how the day can be planned to be flexible and still incorporate this basic guideline.

Be sure to inform parents what happened during the day. If you follow a schedule, you can post it on a bulletin board and include it in your parents' handbook. If you don't follow a schedule, you can list the various activities you have done. Maybe you will keep running notes about what the children do, or at least what the younger ones do: "Tesila learned how to put the clothespins in the milk carton today." Parents are usually eager to find out what their children do during the day. Sharing what you do builds communication and helps parents recognize your efforts and respect your perceptions.

Figure 7. Sample daily plan modified from Janet Everingham's schedule

Approximate time	Possible activities
7:30 a.m.	Arrive, free play. Children help prepare breakfast and lunch.
9:00	Eat breakfast. Discuss plans for the day. Clean up from breakfast. Change diapers, use toilet. Brush teeth.
9:50	Table activities: art, puzzles, beads, small blocks, cooking, nature study.
10:30	Free play. Music/movement activities. Outdoor play (on porch in bad weather).
11:30	Watch *Mister Rogers* and prepare lunch.
12:00 noon	Eat lunch. Clean up. Change diapers, use toilet. Brush teeth. Read stories.
1:00 p.m.	Nap time. Provider's break.
2:30	Wake up and cuddle time, one by one. Eat snack. Change diapers, use toilet. Free play indoors or out.
4:30	Pick up toys, get ready to go home. Stories.

Activities

Your choice of activities will be influenced by the developmental levels of the children in your home. The idea behind this important concept is that children play in different ways depending on

- their experiences and interests,
- their ages, and
- their special needs.

One 2-year-old might climb better than another 4-year-old. A younger child who has played with a material frequently will use it in more complex ways than an older child who has not had any experience with that material.

Provide many chances for children to make **real** choices (such as which song to sing) and explore ideas (as in dramatic play) or objects (an old clock or blocks, for example) on their own. Young children learn by handling real-life materials. **Lectures and worksheets have no place in early childhood education.** Allow enough time for each activity, so children do not feel pressured, but have time to see each activity to completion.

Help children do what they are interested in, and offer materials and assistance in a way that helps them learn to help themselves. Your biggest job is to encourage children, to give them a sense of self-respect and accomplishment. They need room to try out and use their abilities. You can support them by encouraging their efforts (rather than praising their results) and providing them the opportunity and materials they need to develop in the ways they choose. A good child care provider watches individual children for signs of what activities appeal to them. One child might love to climb, another to build, another to make music, and another to act out family roles. Your challenge is to help all of them grow; to learn about themselves, others, and the world; and to feel good about what they can do and who they are in this world. Curious, confident children will continue to be eager learners and cooperative people.

Presenting activities. Present toys and materials in different ways to stimulate children's play. For instance, water play is a wonderful activity for children of any age, assuming you have a good setup and a few simple rules. One day you might add containers for pouring in the dish pans or water table. Another day you might prepare warm, soapy water and bubble makers. Another day the children might bathe the baby dolls, or wash the cars and trucks. Then one day, there is snow to play in, or children can paste Styrofoam packing pieces.

Similarly, painting with tempera paints is a favorite activity for children aged 2 and older. One day the children might paint on tissue paper, allowing the colors to bleed together. Another day they could make

R. Mullin

Provide many chances for children to make real choices (such as which song to sing) and explore ideas (as in dramatic play) or objects (an old clock or blocks, for example) on their own.

note cards from construction paper. Another day school-age children might use crayons first, and then paint with water colors over the top, to see how the wax resists the paint.

How you present an activity will vary by the children's developmental levels and the mood of the moment. Suppose you want to set up an art activity with discarded magazines, scissors, paste, and paper. Older children may be able to select the pictures they want to use, cut them out, and paste them on their paper without any help. You may be needed only to set up the materials, and perhaps to keep them company. A younger child may need a lot of help learning how to use scissors, and in fact the cutting may turn out to be the

whole activity. You might decide to skip the gluing part with that child, and offer an envelope to hold the precious cuttings instead. An even younger child might simply turn the pages, looking at the pictures as you describe them. A baby might watch and be talked to, or be entertained by an older child as she or he works or by one who finishes the project first. Or you might want to wait to do this activity with the older ones after the younger children are asleep.

Try to avoid focusing on the end product of children's activities—it is the **doing** of them, the process, that is important to young children. Each child's work should be different—not all made from the same pattern or by coloring in some adult's idea of what an object looks like. Involve the children in every step of the process. You will waste your time, and the children's time, if you do most of the project yourself just so everyone's work looks neat.

Depending on the ages of the children, you might want to do an activity all together, with a small group, or individually. Let the children know you value the younger children's work as much as the older children's. Show the toddler's mother the envelope full of the child's cut out magazine pictures. Avoid doing activities just to impress parents. As a professional, you will want to keep your program child-centered at all times. Explain to parents why it is important for children to invest themselves in their work. Watch how proud and confident children are when they say "I did it all by myself!"

Children need unstructured, experimenting time, especially when they try a new toy or material. For instance, Kathy noticed that a group of children who were not familiar with clay wanted to play with it every chance they got. So she put it out twice a day for as long as they were interested, which turned out to be 2 weeks for two of the children. During that time they did not need any activity suggestions from her, although they shared many ideas with

Nancy P. Alexander

Your biggest job is to encourage children, to give them a sense of self-respect and accomplishment.

each other. After this experimentation period was over, they were ready for variations such as plastic knives, rolling dowels, and cookie cutters.

As children become familiar with the possibilities and more advanced in skill, you can facilitate more complex play. Combine materials and equipment in different ways. Some teachers like to put out activities in threes, such as clay, sea shells, and coffee stirrers; or wooden blocks, farm animals, and construction paper and scissors. Whatever the project, make sure it is the children, not you, who do it. Your role is to set the stage for their involved learning and pleasure.

The emotional climate

The other half of your program, beside the activities, is the emotional part — what it feels like to be in your home and in the group. Children form their opinions of themselves based on what important peo-

ple in their early years feel about them. They learn to treat others as they are treated. Children who have never felt safe must learn to trust others before they can be independent. Children who have been criticized a lot need to be encouraged and to feel successful before they will learn to explore. Here are some things you can do to help children feel good about themselves and others.

Discipline and guiding behavior. Develop a few rules, appropriate for the ages of children in the group, about getting along together and caring for materials. State the rules in simple, positive terms that are understood by all. Be consistent about asking all children to follow the rules, adjusting for age differences. If you explain in a relaxed, friendly way that "this is the way it is here," most children will quickly learn to live within these guidelines. Remember, the purpose of discipline is to help children learn to control their own behavior.

52

The idea of discipline does not apply to babies. In fact, if you are strict or stingy with a baby, that child is likely to become more demanding. There is a saying "If you baby the baby, you won't have to baby the toddler." It does not make sense to talk about spoiling babies. Babies who have been picked up and carried a lot are less likely to want to be overly pampered as older children. If you respond to babies' cries quickly when they are very young, they will cry less when they are older. Watch babies for clues about what they need, or when they have had too much stimulation, or when they are bored. Let babies guide your behavior!

For toddlers, prevention and distraction are the major techniques of discipline. If there are interesting activities, enough toys, and a child-paced schedule, toddlers will usually stay busy and happy. Try to set up your space so that you never have to say "No, no, don't touch that." Prevent trouble before it happens. Distract children from unacceptable behavior. Toddlers will share when they are ready—a concept you may have to explain to parents, who often expect young babies to share with others. When you are generous with children— with your time and with ample materials —they will soon become generous with each other.

Have respect for and faith in each child. Use encouragement and good examples to build positive behavior. Punishment and criticism will not necessarily eliminate negative behavior, and they will cause other problems. Remember, the children

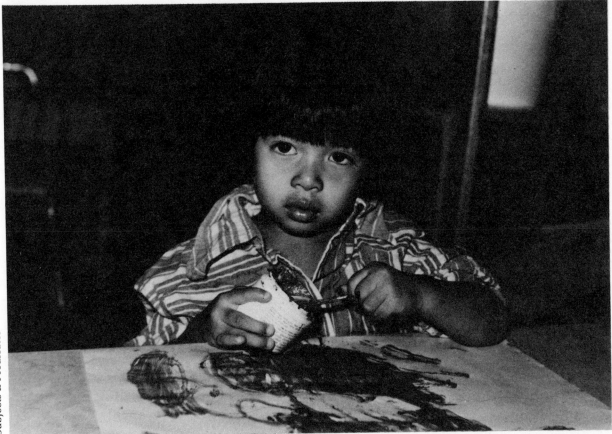

Try to avoid focusing on the end product of children's activities—it is the doing of them, the process, that is important to young children. Each child's work should be different—not all made from the same pattern or by coloring in some adult's idea of what an object looks like.

53

If you are strict or stingy with a baby, that child is likely to become more demanding.

will imitate people who are important to them. Ignore attention-getting misbehavior when you can, but pay lots of careful attention to each child at other times. If you find that you do not like a child, work to change your feelings by finding something about that individual that you do like, and expand on it. Whenever possible, ignore what you don't like.

Do not get into a power struggle with a child. Instead, be firm but also kind and trustworthy. Give the child a chance to be helpful to you and the other children, to make choices, and to be successful.

Create an atmosphere that is pleasant for you and the children. Examine negative feelings for what can be done to improve the situation. Do not allow constant fighting—separate the fighters until they are ready to cooperate or at least ignore each other. If a child cries a lot, work actively to get to the bottom of the problem. If you find yourself chronically short-tem-

pered, work to eliminate the causes of your frustration and to feel more cheerful.

On the other hand, there is nothing wrong with occasional honest expression of anger, and there is nothing wrong with a heated argument between two children trying to resolve a conflict. In fact, you should encourage children to say what they are thinking—to each other—at these times. But when someone feels bad a lot of the time—sad, mad, frustrated, or afraid—it is a signal that help is needed.

Your program can help children learn and grow to be happy, productive people. What you do every minute will help shape the adults of tomorrow. Enjoy your work as a professional!

Reference

National Association for the Education of Young Children. (1985). *Toys: Tools for learning.* Washington, DC: NAEYC.

PART 5. YOU AS A PROFESSIONAL

——————— Training ———————

Providers often begin with no training, other than that of being a parent or a baby-sitter. But most providers find that caring for a group of children presents more challenges than their experience has prepared them to meet. Therefore, you may find that training in early childhood education and child development are very useful to your work. It is surprising how much can be learned about positive ways to discipline or guide children, or types of activities for different developmental levels. Many of us who came to child care after our children had grown wish that we could have had the benefit of training before we had our own children!

Research has shown that provider training is related to the quality of child care. Trained providers are more in demand by parents, who are becoming increasingly sophisticated about selecting care for their children. Where can you go to get more training in your profession?

Academic courses and preparation for state teacher certification are offered by many 2- and 4-year colleges and universities. Training series or individual workshops may be offered by resource and referral agencies, NAEYC Affiliate Groups, adult education programs, or school districts.

The Child Development Associate Program

The Child Development Associate (CDA) Program is one form of training available to family day care providers. The Child Development Associate program offers a national credential based on performance with children and families. By participat-

ing in this process you can learn more about your work and be recognized for your skills. The competency standards for the credential can help you identify your strengths and weaknesses, even if you do not apply for the program. The cognitive competency area is presented in Figure 8 to give you an idea of how practical and valuable the CDA process can be. For further information about this voluntary program, or a copy of the book containing all the competencies identified for family day care providers, call the Council for Early Childhood Professional Recognition at 202-265-9090 or 800-424-4310.

Larry Pakyz · Photo Graphics

Trained providers are more in demand by parents.

55

Figure 8. CDA Functional Area: Cognitive

This is one of 13 functional areas in which competencies have been identified for family day care providers. For further information about this voluntary program, or a copy of the book containing all the competencies, call the Council for Early Childhood Professional Recognition at 202-265-9090 or 800-424-4310.

Candidate provides activities and opportunities that encourage curiosity, exploration, and problem solving appropriate to the developmental levels and learning styles of children.

DEVELOPMENTAL CONTEXT

Exploring and trying to understand the world is natural and necessary for children's cognitive or intellectual development. As children learn and grow, their thinking capacities expand and become more flexible. Adults should support and guide this process by responding to children's interests with new learning opportunities and to their questions, with information and enthusiasm. Cognitive growth also requires healthy development in other areas: consistent physical growth, secure emotional behavior, and positive social interaction.

Young infants (birth to 9 months) begin cognitive or intellectual learning through their interactions with caring adults in a secure environment. Some of their early learning includes becoming familiar with distance and space relationships, sounds, similarity and differences among things, and visual perspectives from various positions (front, back, under, and over).

Mobile infants (6 to 18 months) actively learn through trying things out; using objects as tools; comparing; imitating; looking for lost objects; and naming familiar objects, places, and people. By giving them opportunities to explore space, objects, and people and by sharing children's pleasure in discovery, adults can build children's confidence in their ability to learn and understand.

Toddlers (16 to 36 months) enter into a new and expansive phase of mental activity. They are beginning to think in words and symbols, remember, and imagine. Their curiosity leads them to try out materials in many ways, and adults can encourage this natural interest by providing a variety of new materials for experimentation. Adults can create a supportive social environment for learning by showing enthusiasm for children's individual discoveries and by helping them use words to describe and understand their experiences.

Preschool children (3 through 5 years), as well as toddlers, continue cognitive growth through actively exploring and manipulating real objects, imitating adults and other children in a variety of roles, and repeating and practicing their learning. Their increasing ability to describe objects and experiences with words reinforces their understanding of abstract concepts. Adults can expand learning through play, introduce a variety of new opportunities for learning, and ensure that preschoolers experience a balance of challenge and success.

For example, the competent Candidate working with infants and toddlers and preschool children:

• observes children's play frequently to assess their cognitive development and readiness for new learning opportunities.

• uses techniques and activities that stimulate children's curiosity, inventiveness, and problem-solving and communication skills.

• gives children time and space for extended concentrated play and adjusts routines and schedules for this purpose.

• provides opportunities for children to try out and begin to understand the relationships between cause and effect and means and ends.

• understands the importance of play and often joins children's play as a partner and facilitator.

• uses the home environment, everyday activities, and homemade materials to encourage children's intellectual development.

• helps children discover ways to solve problems that arise in daily activities.

• supports children's repetitions of the familiar and introduces new experiences, activities, and materials when children are interested and ready.

• recognizes differences in individual learning styles and finds ways to work effectively with each child.

• encourages active learning rather than emphasizing adult talking and children's passive listening.

• obtains (or makes) and uses special learning materials and equipment for children whose handicaps affect their ability to learn.

The competent Candidate working with **young infants** also, for example:

• talks to infants, describing what they feel, hear, touch, and see.

• encourages manipulation and inspection of a variety of objects.

• provides opportunities for infants to interact with adults and children and watch interactions of adults and children.

• encourages infants in imitating others.

• plays with infants frequently.

The competent Candidate working with **mobile infants** also, for example:

• talks, sings, plays with, and reads to mobile infants.

• gives children more space to explore as they become more mobile.

• gives children many opportunities to figure out cause and effect, how things work.

• provides many experiences with moving, hiding, and changing objects.

The competent Candidate working with **toddlers** also, for example:

• encourages children to ask questions and seek help and responds to them in ways that extend their thinking; for example, ''That's a good question; let's see if we can find out.''

• asks questions that have more than one answer, encouraging children to wonder, guess, and talk about their ideas, such as, ''What do you think might happen if . . .?'' or ''How do you feel when . . .?''

• encourages children to name objects and to talk about their experiences and observations.

• provides opportunities to organize and group, compare and contrast thoughts, words, objects, and sensations.

• involves toddlers in projects such as cooking, gardening, and repairing, when possible.

• reduces distractions and interruptions so that toddlers have opportunities to extend their attention spans and work on one activity, such as block building or water play, for a long period of time.

The competent Candidate working with **preschool children** also, for example:

• stimulates exploration, comparing, wondering, and experimentation through materials, conversations, and activities.

• helps children understand concepts such as space, time, shape, and quantity through many different activities.

• uses field trips as opportunities to expand children's knowledge and understanding of their world, when possible.

In addition, the competent Candidate working towards the **bilingual specialization,** for example:

• provides learning experiences that lead to the understanding of basic concepts in the language most familiar to each child.

• encourages learning of both languages through everyday experiences and activities.

Some people are able to train themselves just by reading books such as those listed in the Bibliography. Some people learn the most from visiting child care homes and talking to other providers. The idea is for you to keep learning, in whatever way you can. New ideas and information will be an asset in your work with children.

CDA Competency Goals and Functional Areas for family day care providers

Competency Goal I: To establish and maintain a safe, healthy, learning environment

   1. Safe
   2. Healthy
   3. Learning Environment

Competency Goal II: To advance physical and intellectual competence

   4. Physical
   5. Cognitive
   6. Communication
   7. Creative

Competency Goal III: To support social and emotional development and provide positive guidance

   8. Self
   9. Social
   10. Guidance

Competency Goal IV: To establish positive and productive relationships with families

   11. Families

Competency Goal V: To ensure a well-run, purposeful program responsive to participant needs

   12. Program management

Competency Goal VI: To maintain a commitment to professionalism

   13. Professionalism

Reprinted from *Child Development Associate Assessment System and Competency Standards: Family Day Care Providers*, 1983, pages 3-4, by permission of the Council for Early Childhood Professional Recognition, 1718 Connecticut Ave., N.W., Washington, DC 20009.

Getting support

Being a home-based child care provider is rewarding—but it is also hard work. It takes a lot of energy, and you may feel isolated from other adults. It helps a lot to belong to a group of providers who have many of the same interests and problems you encounter. In many communities there is a family day care association. In others, the local Affiliate of NAEYC includes home child care providers. Your nearest child care referral agency will probably be able to tell you what exists in your community.

Many providers find it helpful to have a partner, someone they can call about any problem, for advice, or just to let off steam. Having a support group of providers will give you confidence in the decisions you make. The group will reinforce your feeling of being a child care professional when you talk to parents. And it will keep you from feeling isolated, which is one of the worst occupational hazards of this work. Some providers like to make sure they have frequent visitors who will appreciate and respond to what is happening in their child care group.

You can also belong to NAEYC and take advantage of the high quality conferences and workshops they provide at the county, state, and national levels. In addition, every other month you will receive the journal *Young Children*. It will help you keep up with the newest developments and give you great activity ideas. Many books, brochures, posters, and videotapes are also available from NAEYC, including some you may want to share with parents on topics such as discipline, toy selection, infant care, and helping children when they enter a new group. Your concerns *are* shared by thousands of other early childhood professionals across the country.

Occasionally, a provider's job can be very difficult. Perhaps you may discover a case of child abuse among your families—or one of the children's parents might die. Or you might feel that you are losing control of yourself in your frustration with an infant who won't stop crying. At times like this, it is especially important to get the best help available in your community, so that you can do your best in handling the situation. You, as a professional, have a big job to do, especially when a crisis occurs. After it is over, when you have met the challenge, you may feel that it was among the most gratifying experiences in your life.

In addition to finding outside support for yourself, you should make sure *you* respect what you do and take care of your own needs. Learn successful child guidance techniques so that you can make your home's atmosphere pleasant for yourself as well as the children—you are going to be spending your days there, too! Let your own family members know what you need and how you feel—you deserve their support.

Schedule a quiet time for yourself in the middle of and at the end of every day. If at all possible, take an occasional afternoon off, and take vacations. Here again it is important to have a good, regular sub, who can fill in for you. Marie says that 1 week's vacation every 6 months is essential for her. If you keep yourself rested, you will do a better job, as well as enjoy it more.

There are many critical, demanding jobs that go under-recognized in our society. Taking care of children is at the top of that list. People who take care of children should be able to look in the mirror and say, "I know I'm doing something important!" You ARE!

BIBLIOGRAPHY

———— Family day care ————

Administration for Children, Youth and Families. (1981). *Family day care in the United States* (Seven Volumes) (DHHS Publication Nos. OHDS 80-30282 through 80-30287). Washington, DC: U.S. Department of Health and Human Services. Free
    Report of the most comprehensive research study on home child care in the United States. The Executive Summary and Summary of Findings are of particular interest.

Agency for Instructional Television. (1981). *Spoonful of lovin': A manual for day care providers.* Box A, Bloomington, IN 47402. $11.95
    Practical guide for family day care; designed for group training or individual self-study. May be used with related videotape series (see Audiovisual Materials section).

Alston, Francis Kemper. (1984). *Caring for other people's children: A complete guide to family day care.* University Park Press, 300 N. Charles St., Baltimore, MD 21201. $14.95

Broad, Laura Peabody & Butterworth, Nancy. (1974). *The playgroup handbook.* St. Martin's Press, 175 Fifth Ave., New York, NY 10010. $7.95

Brown, Jeanne; Hathaway, Irene; & Lueck, Lynn (Eds.). (1982). *Resources for the family day care provider.* Cooperative Extension Service Bulletin E-1593. Washtenaw County Cooperative Extension Service, Box 8645, Ann Arbor, MI 48107. $3
    A basic and comprehensive guide to home child care, with especially useful sections on startup, business management, parent-provider relations, health, food, and interactions with children.

California Child Care Resource and Referral Network. (1986). *Family day care handbook.* California Child Care Initiative, 809 Lincoln Way, San Francisco, CA 94122.
    A compilation of articles from family day care trainers across the country, exploring many relevant topics.

Child Care Law Center. (1986). *Child custody disputes: Who can the child go home with?* 625 Market St., #815, San Francisco, CA 94105. $2.50
    Discusses legal aspects of custody and suggestions for handling difficult situations with divorcing parents.

Child Care Law Center. (1986). *Collecting fees owed: Using small claims court.* 625 Market St., #815, San Francisco, CA 94105. $2.50
    How to sue or threaten to sue a parent who has not paid for child care services.

Child Care Law Center. *Insuring your program: Vehicle and property insurance.* 625 Market St., #815, San Francisco, CA 94105. $2.50
    Survey of the forms of insurance available to licensed and unlicensed providers, with discussion about which are the most important protections.

Child Care Law Center. (1986). *Parent-provider contracts.* 625 Market St., #815, San Francisco, CA 94105. $2.50
    Benefits of using contracts, and how to make a contract. Includes excellent samples.

Child Development Associate National Credentialing Program (1985). *Child Development Associate assessment system and competency standards: Family day care providers.* 1718 Connecticut Ave., N.W., Washington, DC 20009.
    Complete description of the CDA process. See Figure 8 (page 56) for an example of one of the 13 competency standards.

The Children's Foundation. (1986). *Fact sheet on the Child Care Food Program in family day care homes.* 815 15th St., N.W., #928, Washington, DC 20005. $.50
    Pamphlet explains the guidelines for this important source of income and nutrition information for providers.

The Children's Foundation. (1985). *Family day care—Implications for the Black community.* 815 15th St., N.W., #928, Washington, DC 20005. $1.50
    Overview of issues and problems confronting Black providers.

The Children's Foundation. (1986). *National directory of family day care associations.* 815 15th St., N.W., #928, Washington, DC 20005. $5
    Partial list of home-based child care associations by state. Includes section on beginning an association.

Dane County 4-C's. (1974). *Family day care handbook.* 3200 Monroe St., Madison, WI 53704.

Good sections on provider-parent responsibilities, health, child development through age 13, the environment, and activities.

Fish, Debra (Ed.). (1977). *Home-based training resource handbook.* Toys 'n Things Training and Resource Center, 906 N. Dale St., St. Paul, MN 55103. $29.95

A comprehensive resource for trainers, this 394-page book draws on the pioneering work of Kathleen McNellis and Sally Kilmer.

Frank Porter Graham Child Development Center. (1981). *Family day care education series information packets.* University of North Carolina at Chapel Hill. Packets are $1.25 each, or $21.95 for all 13

Each packet contains information, activities for children and caregivers, handouts for parents, free and inexpensive resources, and a user's guide. Titles are: *Family Day Care and You; Day Care as a Small Business; Care for the School-Age Child; Special Things for Special Kids; Planning an Activity Program; Health and Safety; Space to Play and Learn; Community Help for Caregivers; One Land: Many Cultures; Working With Parents; Good Food for Kids; Growth and Development; Handling Behavior Problems.* Trainer's manual and independent study course are also available.

Garcia, Ronda. (1985). *Home centered care: Designing a family day care program.* The Children's Council of San Francisco, 3896 24th St., San Francisco, CA 94114.

A provider presents practical information on setting up your home for infants, toddlers, preschoolers, and school-age children.

Genser, Andrea & Baden, Clifford. (Eds.). (1980). *School-age child care: Programs and issues — Papers from a June 1979 conference at Wheelock College.* (ERIC Document Reproduction Service No. ED 196 543). ERIC/EECE, University of Illinois, College of Education, 805 W. Pennsylvania Ave., Urbana, IL 61801.

Informal papers on a range of issues about school-age care, including fighting, teasing, cruelty, vandalism; homework and tutoring; autonomy and competence. Excellent section on financial management, discussion of evaluation of home programs.

Harms, Thelma; Cryer, Debby; & Bourland, Beth. (1986). *The active learning series.* Menlo Park, CA: Addison-Wesley.

Basic practical activities for working with infants, toddlers, and young preschoolers in groups. Each activity is complete with developmental guidelines.

Hemmings, Mary. (1976). *A handbook for family day care providers: Facts and fantasies.* Quality Child Care, Mound, MN 55364.

A common sense approach to life in home-based child care, with emphasis on program and parent relations.

Murray, Kathleen A., Esq., & Stevenson, Carol S., Esq.; revised by Kell, William, & O'Shea, Lynne. (1985). *Insuring your program: Liability insurance.* Child Care Law Center, 625 Market St., #815, San Francisco, CA 94105. $3

Nash, Maggie & Tate, Costella. (1986). *Better baby care: A book for family day care providers.* The Children's Foundation, 815 15th St., N.W., #928, Washington, DC 20005. $12.95

How babies grow, how they relate to others, how they think. Common behaviors, nutrition, health, and safety. Section on how to prepare your house, room by room.

National Association for the Education of Young Children. (1987). *NAEYC position statement on licensing and regulation of early childhood programs.* 1834 Connecticut Ave., N.W., Washington, DC 20009-5786. $.50 each, $10 for 100

Pamphlet outlining NAEYC's position and rationale for supporting the establishment and implementation of regulations for the care of children outside their own homes.

Overstad, Elizabeth & Fackler, Deborah. (Eds.). (1979). *Potpourri of child care development pamphlets.* Toys 'n Things Press, 906 N. Dale St., St. Paul, MN 55103. $15.95

Topical index of 100 high quality pamphlets from a wide variety of sources. All available free or at low cost. Includes ordering instructions and samples of 20 pamphlets.

Prescott, Elizabeth & Melech, Cynthia. (1975). *Family day care for the school age child.* (ERIC Document Reproduction Service No. ED 151 086). ERIC/EECE, University of Illinois, College of Education, 805 W. Pennsylvania Ave., Urbana, IL 61801.

Rodriguez, Dorothy. (1978). A tool for evaluation of family day care mothers. *Child Welfare, 57* (1), 55–58.

Criteria for providers of high quality care.

Rodriguez, Dorothy & Albert, Marilyn. (1981). Self-evaluation for family day caregivers. *Child Welfare, 60* (4), 263–267.

A self-assessment form that allows trainers to identify providers' needs, design individualized assistance, and plan workshops. One of the resources for the self-evaluation in this handbook.

Save the Children Child Care Support Center. (1987). *Child care food program for family day care: A how-to manual.* 1340 Spring St., #200, Atlanta, GA 30309. $5

Save the Children Child Care Support Center. (1987). *Family day care: An option for rural communities.* 1340 Spring St., #200, Atlanta, GA 30309. $6

Save the Children Child Care Support Center. (1979). *Family day care as a child protection service.* 1340 Spring St., #200, Atlanta, GA 30309. $4
  Explores the use of home child care as a resource for children who are in danger of abuse or neglect.

Save the Children Child Care Support Center. (1978). *Establishing a family day care agency.* 1340 Spring St., #200, Atlanta, GA 30309. $4.25
  Practical suggestions for communities interested in forming an agency to coordinate services and assist providers. Describes eight agencies with various sponsorships, funding sources, administrative design, and support services to providers.

Seefeldt, Carol & Dittmann, Laura. (1975). *Day care: Vol. 9—Family day care.* Washington, DC: U.S. Department of Health, Education and Welfare, Office of Child Development (OHD 73-1054). $5
  A classic, including excellent sections on arranging your home for play, guiding behavior, and communicating with child and parents.

Squibb, Betsy. (1980). *Family day care: How to provide it in your home.* Harvard, MA: Harvard Common Press. $6.95
  Overview of licensing, program, parent relations. Strong, supportive attitudes toward home-based child care as a profession, and toward support networks for providers. Extensive resource section.

Toys 'n Things Press. (1986). *Basic guide to record keeping and taxes.* 906 N. Dale St., St. Paul, MN 55103. $5, annual update $2
  Clear step-by-step instructions for keeping business income and expense records, and for completing federal income tax forms for self-employed persons. Some duplication of material in the *Calendar-Keeper.*

Toys 'n Things Press. *Calendar-keeper.* (Updated yearly). 906 N. Dale St., St. Paul, MN 55103. Small (for groups of about 6 children) $7.50, large (for groups of about 12 children) $12.95
  A favorite resource of many providers, and especially helpful for new providers just learning about the business aspects of home-based child care. Easy-to-use recordkeeping system. Space for monthly attendance records, income and expense records, and a tax worksheet. Monthly activity suggestions.

Toys 'n Things Press. (1983). *Sharing in the caring: Family day care parent-provider agreement packet.* 906 N. Dale St., St. Paul, MN 55103. Sample $3.50; 5 packets $6.95; 11 packets $11.50
  Hints on establishing a good business relationship, a brochure for parents, a sample contract to be completed by provider and parents.

Treadwell, Lujuana Wolfe, Esq.; revised by Kell, William. (1986). *Caring for sick and injured children.* Child Care Law Center, 625 Market St., #815, San Francisco, CA 94105. $2.50
  Legal duties in administering medication, preparing for emergencies, and obtaining medical treatment for children in child care.

Treadwell, Lujuana Wolfe, Esq.; revised by Kell, William; Cohen, Abby J., Esq.; & Stevenson, Carol S., Esq. (1986). *Zoning laws and family day care.* $4
  Discusses issues and options for providers. Suggests advocacy strategies for changing zoning laws.

Utah State University Extension Service. (1972). *A home arranged for learning.* Utah State University, UMC 48, Logan, UT 84322. $.25

Valenstein, Thelma. (1972). *At home with children—A resource book for family day care.* (ERIC Catalog #131). University of Illinois, College of Education, 805 W. Pennsylvania Ave., Urbana, IL 61801. $3.50
  An all-round practical guide. Includes an extensive self-evaluation, activity and equipment ideas.

General child care

Benson, Carolyn & Stenzel, Cathy. (Eds.). (1985). *Who cares for kids? A report on child care providers.* National Commission on Working Women, 1325 G St., N.W., Lower Level, Washington, DC 20005.

Comprehensive statistics and information about child care workers, including a section on home-based child care providers.

Blank, Helen & Wilkins, Amy. (1986). *State child care fact book 1986.* The Children's Defense Fund, 122 C St., N.W., Washington, DC 20001.

Fact sheets summarizing child care public policy in each state, including programs and funding levels (information available varies by state).

Bryant, B., Harris, M., & Newton, D. (1980). *Children and minders.* The High/Scope Press, 600 N. River St., Ypsilanti, MI 48197.

Caldwell, Bettye M., & Hilliard, Asa G. III (1984). *What is quality child care?* NAEYC, 1834 Connecticut Ave., N.W., Washington, DC 20009-5786. $2.50

A comprehensive discussion of the components of high quality care. Raises important issues that are often overlooked. Also available on videos ($39 each).

California Child Care Resource and Referral Network. (1986). *National directory of child care information and referral agencies.* 809 Lincoln Way, San Francisco, CA 94122. $10

Comprehensive list of child care referral agencies. Gives basic information including brief summaries of services offered.

Maryland Committee for Children, Public Policy Committee. (1984). *Care of infants in groups.* The Chocolate Factory, 608 Water St., Baltimore, MD 21202.

Summary of research and discussion of implications for child care, recommendations, child development from birth through 5 years.

McCracken, Janet Brown. (1986). *So many goodbyes: Ways to ease the transition between home and groups for young children.* NAEYC, 1834 Connecticut Ave., N.W., Washington, DC 20009-5786. $.50 each, $10 for 100

Brochure to share with parents on helping children adjust to a new child care program.

Modigliani, Kathy. (1986). *Summary of results of licensing survey.* Unpublished. NAEYC, 1834 Connecticut Ave., N.W., Washington, DC 20009-5786.

Ruopp, Richard; Travers, Jeffrey; Glantz, Fredric; & Coelen, Craig. (1979). *Children at the center; Final report of the National Day Care Study* (Vol. 1). Cambridge, MA: Abt Associates.

The most comprehensive study on child care in the United States, presenting some of the best data available. The study measured the components of high quality care.

Rutter, Michael. (1981, January). Social-emotional consequences of day care for preschool children, *American Journal of Orthopsychiatry.* 4–28.

Scheffler, Hannah N. (1983). *Resources for early childhood: An annotated bibliography for educators, librarians, health care professionals and parents.* New York: Garland Press.

U.S. Bureau of the Census. (1983). *Child care arrangements of working mothers: June 1982.* Current Population Reports, Special Studies Series P-23, No. 129. Washington, DC: U.S. Bureau of the Census.

Program Ideas

Blau, Rosalie; Brady, Elizabeth H.; Bucher, Ida; Hiteshew, Betsy; Zavitkovsky, Ann; & Zavitkovsky, Docia. (1977). *Activities for school-age child care.* NAEYC, 1834 Connecticut Ave., N.W., Washington, DC 20009-5786. $4

A wide variety of popular activities for elementary school-aged children.

Butler, A.L., Gotts, E.E., & Quisenberry, N.L. (1978). *Play as development.* Columbus, OH: Merrill. $6.95

Describes the central role of play in a young child's learning. Suggests good answers to the question "Do you just let the kids play all day?"

Cherry, Clare. (1972). *Creative art for the developing child: A teacher's handbook for early childhood education.* Belmont, CA: Fearon. $7.50

A variety of art activities with practical instructions for setup and presentation. Discussion of child development as it pertains to a child's art.

Cherry, Clare. (1968). *Creative movement for the developing child.* Belmont, CA: Fearon. $6.95

    Similar to Cherry's art book. Contains an interesting discussion of the philosophy of teaching children to relax and reduce their own stress.

Council on Interracial Books for Children. *Ten quick ways to analyze children's books for racism and sexism.* 1841 Broadway, New York, NY 10023. $2.95 for 10 copies

    Brochure lists simple steps to assess racist and sexist attitudes in books and other materials. Useful for teaching children how to analyze stereotypes, lifestyles, relationships, and language.

Flemming, Bonnie Mack; Hamilton, Darlene Softley; & Hicks, JoAnne Deal. (1977). *Resources for creative teaching in early childhood education.* New York: Harcourt Brace Jovanovich.

    Activity chapters on self-concept, sensory development, families, holidays including some multicultural focus, the seasons, animal study, transportation, and the world around us.

Friends of Perry Nursery School. (1972). *The scrap book.* Perry Nursery School, 1541 Washtenaw, Ann Arbor, MI 48104. $3.50

    Teacher-chosen activities for young children, including art, cooking, large and small motor activities, and much more.

Hirsch, Elisabeth S. (Ed.). (1984). *The block book* (rev. ed.). NAEYC, 1834 Connecticut Ave., N.W., Washington, DC 20009-5786. $7

    Explores the many kinds of learning in block play—science, art, math, social relations. Covers the development of block play from toddlers through elementary school-aged children. This book will never become obsolete. *A Classroom With Blocks,* a companion filmstrip, is available for $25. The set is $28.

Linderman, C. Emma. *Teachables from trashables.* (1979). Toys 'n Things Press, 906 N. Dale St., St. Paul, MN 55103. $9.95

    Simple directions to make toys from household junk. Suggests activities and discusses the learning that occurs when a child plays with the toys described.

McDonald, Dorothy T. (1979). *Music in our lives: The early years.* NAEYC, 1834 Connecticut Ave., N.W., Washington, DC 20009-5786. $3.50

    Guidelines for teaching music to children from infancy through the preschool years. Lists of songs and records.

National Association for the Education of Young Children. (1985). *Toys: Tools for learning.* NAEYC, 1834 Connecticut Ave., N.W., Washington, DC 20009-5786. $.50 each, $10 for 100

    Tips for selecting appropriate toys for young children.

Pitcher, Evelyn Goodenough; Lasher, Miriam G.; Feinburg, Sylvia G.; & Braun, Linda Abrams. (1979). *Helping young children learn* (3rd ed.). Columbus, OH: Merrill.

    Excellent activity ideas based on self-direction and self-expression. How children learn and what teachers can do to facilitate play and learning. Long sections on art, music, and literature, including theory as well as practical information. Briefer sections on water play, cooking, blocks, carpentry, pets, and more.

UCLA Child Care Services. (1984). *Family day care resource cards.* Children's Book and Music Center, 2500 Santa Monica Blvd., Santa Monica, CA 90404. $15

    Program ideas and curriculum resources for new providers.

Child development

Brazelton, T. Berry. (1983). *Infants and mothers: Differences in development* (rev. ed.). Delta/Seymour, Dell, 1 Dag Hammarskjold Plaza, New York, NY 10017. $10.95

    This popular pediatrician describes different types of babies—how they behave and tips for how to get along best with them. An important reference for infant caregivers.

Brazelton, T. Berry. (1976). *Toddlers and parents: A declaration of independence.* Delacorte Press, Dell, 1 Dag Hammarskjold Plaza, New York, NY 10017. $9.95

    Brazelton helps us appreciate toddler behaviors that might otherwise exasperate us. A comprehensive guide to understanding children of this age.

Brazelton, T. Berry. (1985). *Working and caring.* Reading, MA: Addison-Wesley. $16.95
Explores the psychological issues of parents who choose child care for their infants and toddlers. Particularly useful are the sections on the steps in the developing parent-infant relationship and suggestions for choosing and adjusting to child care.

Comer, James P., & Poussaint, Alvin F. (1976). *Black child care—How to bring up a healthy Black child in America: A guide to emotional and psychological development.* New York: Simon & Schuster. $11.95
Excellent discussion of common concerns, with advice for helping children learn positive ways to deal with racism.

Crary, Elizabeth. (1979). *Without spanking or spoiling: A practical approach to toddler and preschool guidance.* Parenting Press, 7750 31st Ave. N.E., Seattle, WA 98115. $7.95
Clear, practical ideas including a basic introduction to Parent Effectiveness Training (PET), the Dreikurs Approach (STEP), Transactional Analysis, and Behavior Modification. Specific examples and how-to instructions, relevant to toddlers as well as older children.

Crary, Elizabeth. (1984). *Kids can cooperate: A practical guide to teaching problem solving.* Parenting Press, 7750 31st Ave., N.E., Seattle, WA 98115. $7.95
Simple suggestions for helping children learn to resolve their own problems. Builds self-esteem and social skills. This method is so successful that children take it home and introduce it to their families.

Dittmann, Laura L. (Ed.). (1984). *The infants we care for.* NAEYC, 1834 Connecticut Ave., N.W., Washington, DC 20009-5786. $3.50
Includes a chapter on home child care programs.

Fein, Greta G. (1978). *Child development.* Englewood Cliffs, NJ: Prentice-Hall. $14.95
A basic textbook of development from before birth through adolescence.

Fraiberg, Selma H. (1959). *The magic years: Understanding and handling the problems of early childhood.* New York: Scribner's. $7.95
A classic discussion of early child development from a lightly psychoanalytic point of view. Inspires adult appreciation of the magical thinking and critical issues of young children at different ages.

Hendrick, Joanne. (1986). *Total learning: Curriculum for the young child.* Columbus, OH: Merrill. $26.95
The basics of early childhood education presented as a down-to-earth, child-centered approach: nutrition, safety, physical development, fostering emotional health, developing social competence, creativity, language and cognitive development, working with parents, and recordkeeping. A favorite textbook.

Jones, Elizabeth & Prescott, Elizabeth. (1979). *Supporting the growth of infants, toddlers and parents.* Pasadena, CA: Pacific Oaks College.

McCall, Robert B. (1979). *Infants.* Cambridge, MA: Harvard University Press. $10
Basic review of the practical implications of research on infant development.

—— Journals and newsletters ——

Several other newsletters are listed in the Appendix.

Beginnings: Books for Teachers of Young Children. Exchange Press, P.O. Box 2890, Redmond, WA 98073.
Full of interesting and useful information. Each quarterly book explores a particular issue or curriculum topic, and includes program ideas, child development, teacher development, and resources.

Child Care Resources. Child Care Fair, P.O. Box 324, Mound, MN 55364. $15 per year
Monthly training publication for home child care providers.

Family Day Care Exchange. Cooperative Extension Service, Publications Distribution, Iowa State University, Ames, IA 50011. $4.50 per set

Package of 12 newsletters focusing on a variety of home child care program issues. Geared to providers.

Family Day Care Bulletin. The Children's Foundation, 815 15th St., #928, Washington, DC 20005.
Newsletter written for providers. Information, current issues, association news, and program ideas.

School Age NOTES. P.O. Box 120674, Nashville, TN 37212.
Bimonthly newsletter for providers who work with elementary school children.

Totline. Totline Press, P.O. Box 2255, Everett, WA 98203. $12 per year
Bimonthly activity newsletter for family child care providers.

Audiovisual materials

Bank Street's Family Day Care Cassettes. (1986). Bank Street College, 610 W. 112th St., New York, NY 10025. $15 each (plus $2 postage and handling per order)

A series of 30-minute tapes and accompanying booklets specifically for home-based child care providers to use on their own or in groups. Content is based on the Child Development Associate (CDA) Competencies for Family Child Care Providers (see page 56.) A joint project of Bank Street College of Education, The Child Care Action Campaign, and John Merrow Productions.

KRMA TV: Denver Public Schools, & Mile High Child Care Association of Denver. (1981). *Spoonful of lovin'*. Agency for Instructional Television, Box A, Bloomington, IN 47402.

A video series of five 30-minute programs, coordinated with a book of the same name (see listing for Agency for Instructional Television in Home-Based Child Care section of this bibliography). Especially useful for child development issues and income tax information. Explores day-to-day issues facing providers — good discussion starters.

Texas Department of Human Resources. (1977). *Infant and day home care*. Media Services Division 151-X, Texas Department of Human Resources, P.O. Box 2960, Austin, TX 78769. 20 modules, $40/module

Toys 'n Things Press. (1980). *Inviting spaces* and *Make room for children*. 906 N. Dale St., St. Paul, MN 55103. $34.50 each

Two filmstrips with audible signal cassette tapes, focusing on setting up and using a good family child care environment. The first filmstrip presents and in-depth look at the physical environment; the second focuses on the effects of home child care on the provider's family.

Book Distributors

AFRO-AM Distributing Co. 819 South Wabash Ave., #610, Chicago, IL 60605. 312-922-1147.

Offers a wide range of curriculum materials, teaching guides, and supplemental kits to enhance Black cultural awareness. Free catalog.

The Children's Small Press Collection. Kathy Baxter, 719 N. Fourth Ave., Ann Arbor, MI 48104. 313-668-8056.

National Association for the Education of Young Children. 1834 Connecticut Ave., N.W., Washington, DC 20009-5786. 202-232-8777 or 800-424-2460.

Resources for Child Caring, Inc. 906 N. Dale St., St. Paul, MN 55103. 612-488-7284.

Distributes books, training guides, audiovisual materials, including all materials of Toys 'n Things Press. Free catalog.

APPENDIX: NATIONAL ORGANIZATIONS

Child Care Action Campaign
99 Hudson St., #1233
New York, NY 10013
212-334-9595
A coalition of leaders from diverse organizations advocating for high quality child care. Activities include education, information service, proposing possible solutions, and technical assistance to governmental offices. Publishes bimonthly newsletter. Individual membership $20.

The Child Care Employee Project
P.O. Box 5603
Berkeley, CA 94705
415-653-9889
A clearinghouse on child care employee issues including salaries, status, and working conditions. Publications on such topics as comparable worth/job discrimination, personnel policies. Newsletter, $5 by subscription.

The Child Care Food Program (CCFP)
U.S. Department of Agriculture
Washington, DC 20250
Sponsors nutrition education and reimburses partial food costs to family day care and center child care programs—a specific amount for each child per meal or snack. If your state licenses programs, contact your local licensing office to find sponsors for your area. Otherwise, contact your state department of agriculture or education.

The Child Care Law Center
624 Market St., #815
San Francisco, CA 94105
415-495-5498
Extensive information and assistance in legal and business aspects of home-based child care.

The Children's Defense Fund
122 C St., N.W.
Washington, DC 20001
202-628-8787
800-424-9602
Education about and advocacy for the needs of children, especially low-income, minority, and handicapped children. Publications include a monthly newsletter on federal legislation and an annual analysis of the federal budget. Call for free publications catalog.

The Children's Foundation
815 15th St., N.W., #928
Washington, DC 20005
202-347-3300
Information and materials on home-based child care issues. Publishes the *Family Day Care Bulletin* and *Directory of Family Day Care Associations*. Sponsors the National Family Child Care Advocacy Project and a resource clearinghouse. Sample newsletter and publications list available upon request.

Cooperative Extension Service
Located in local county government offices
Free and inexpensive materials on home child care, child development, and other topics of interest to providers. Look in the white pages of your phone book under your county's name (for example: Washtenaw County Government —Cooperative Extension Service).

Council for Early Childhood Professional Recognition
1718 Connecticut Ave., N.W.
Washington, DC 20009
202-265-9090
800-424-4310
Purpose is to train, assess the competence of, and certify caregivers. Awards credentials to home-based child care providers, preschool and infant-toddler caregivers, and home visitors. Bilingual specialization also available. The competencies for home-based child care providers are listed on page 58. They are useful for self-evaluation and to identify areas for further development.

ERIC Clearinghouse on Elementary and Early Childhood Education (ERIC/EECE)
College of Education
University of Illinois
805 W. Pennsylvania Ave.
Urbana, IL 61801-4877
217-333-1386
Publishes four newsletters yearly on materials, publications, and events. $5 per year. Computer searches on any early childhood topic (ask your local librarian for more information).

Mothers at Home
9673 Lee Highway
Fairfax, VA 22031
703-352-2292
Supports mothers who choose to work at home. Publishes monthly newsletter, *Welcome Home*. Membership $12.

National Association for the Education of Young Children (NAEYC)
1834 Connecticut Ave., N.W.
Washington, DC 20009-5786
202-232-8777
800-424-2460
The largest professional group of early childhood educators/child care providers. Publishes the journal *Young Children*, brochures, posters, videotapes, and books. National, state, and local Affiliate Groups offer training opportunities. Other programs are the Information Service and the Week of the Young Child.

National Black Child Development Institute
1463 Rhode Island Ave., N.W.
Washington, DC 20005
202-387-1281
Publishes a newsletter and calendar featuring issues and important dates in history relevant to the development of Black children.

National Center for Clinical Infant Programs
733 15th St., N.W., #912
Washington, DC 20005
202-347-0308
Publishes information and sponsors conferences on infant health, mental health, and development.

National Commission on Working Women
1325 G St., N.W., Lower Level
Washington, DC 20005
202-737-5764
Focuses on the needs and concerns of the approximately 80% of women in the work force who are concentrated in low-paying, low-status jobs. Excellent work on child care employees (see Benson and Stentzel in the General Child Care section of the Bibliography).

Resources for Child Caring
906 North Dale St.
St. Paul, MN 55103
612-488-7284
Publishes books, training guides, audio-visual materials. Includes Toys 'n Things Press. Write for free catalog.

Save the Children Child Care Support Center
1340 Spring St., N.W., #200
Atlanta, GA 30309
404-885-1578
Sponsors yearly conference for home-based child care providers. Publications include a guide to home-based child care audio-visual training resources.

School-Age Child Care Project
Wellesley College
Center for Research on Women
Wellesley, MA 02181
617-431-1453
Clearinghouse publishes *School-Age Child Care* newsletter.

Toys 'n Things Press. See Resources for Child Caring.

Work and Family Information Center
The Conference Board
845 Third Ave.
New York, NY 10022
212-759-0900
Clearinghouse for information concerning interrelationship between work and family; and employer-supported child care, including resource and referral services, family day care satellites, and parent fee subsidies.

NAEYC is . . .

. . . a membership-supported organization of people committed to fostering the growth and development of children from birth through age 8. Membership is open to all who share a desire to serve and act on behalf of the needs and rights of young children.

NAEYC provides . . .

. . . educational services and resources to adults who work with and for children, including

- *Young Children,* the Journal for early childhood educators
- **Books, posters, brochures, and videos** to expand professional knowledge and commitment to young children, with topics including infants, curriculum, research, discipline, teacher education, and parent involvement
- An **Annual Conference** that brings people from all over the country to share their expertise and advocate on behalf of children and families
- **Week of the Young Child** celebrations sponsored by NAEYC Affiliate Groups across the nation to call public attention to the needs and rights of children and families
- **Insurance plans** for individuals and programs
- **Public policy information** for knowledgeable advocacy efforts at all levels of government
- The **National Academy of Early Childhood Programs,** a voluntary accreditation system for high quality programs for children
- The **Information Service,** a computerized, central source of information sharing, distribution, and collaboration

For free information about membership, publications, or other NAEYC services . . . call NAEYC at 202-232-8777 or 800-424-2460 or write to NAEYC, 1834 Connecticut Avenue, N.W., Washington, DC 20009-5786.